"Greg Cagle has been my executive coach, my friend, and at times, the person I "coach" right back, which is exactly how the best relationships work. His ability to ask the question I didn't know I needed, to challenge the patterns I couldn't see, and to create space for transformation has shaped not just my leadership, but my life. This book is Greg at his best: vulnerable, practical, and profoundly human, inviting us all to stop surviving our circumstances and start bending reality toward who we're called to become."

Cullen Barbato,
CEO of United Fitness Partners

"In all the time I have known Greg Cagle, he has never failed to challenge my thinking or add value to my life. And now, with the help of Reality Benders, he is going to do the same for you. In these pages, Greg will move you from passive participation in life to intentional leadership. You won't just gain new ideas; you'll gain a new lens for living and leading."

Perry Holley,
Executive Coach, Maxwell Leadership

"Greg Cagle has been my executive coach for nearly ten years, and his impact on my leadership has been profound. He taught me to recognize my blind spots, to respond rather than react, and to navigate organizational dynamics with a level of emotional intelligence I wouldn't have developed on my own. Greg challenges you to dig deep and invest in yourself, and he earns the right to make that challenge because he genuinely cares. *Reality Benders* captures the wisdom that has made him not just an exceptional coach, but a trusted friend."

Johnny McKellar,
President, Hendrick Autoguard & NationsGuard

REALITY BENDERS

HARNESS THE **POWER OF EMOTION,** UNLOCK **INFINITE POSSIBILITIES,** & REIGNITE YOUR **IMAGINATION**

GREG CAGLE

Illustrations by Jesse Barnett

To my wife.

Before this book ever existed, there was you.

There were your quiet sacrifices that no one saw.

Your patience when life felt uncertain.

Your encouragement when I questioned myself.

*Your belief in me, especially in the moments
when I didn't have enough belief of my*

own.

*You have stood beside me through every version
of who I've been, loving me not only*

for who I was, but for who I was still becoming.

Because of you, my life is not just successful, it is meaningful.

Not just full, but deeply rich with love and purpose.

*What we have built together is the greatest
reality I could have ever imagined.*

I am better because of you.

I am stronger because of you.

*And I am endlessly grateful that I get to
walk through this life with you.*

CONTENTS

UNLOCKING THE MIND THAT SHAPES YOUR WORLD

hat if your entire life—every result you've produced, every breakthrough you've missed, every loop you can't seem to escape,wasn't just happening *to* you, but was being shaped *by* you? Not by accident, but by a hidden process you've been running every day … without even knowing it?

Everything you've believed about "reality",the things you think are just the way they are—is up for renegotiation. Because reality isn't fixed; it's flexible. It *bends*. What if *you* could actually reshape it into the life you want to live?

It isn't magic—it's what a **Reality Bender** does.

A Reality Bender doesn't just accept life "as is." They consciously mold it, reframing circumstances, outcomes, and even other people's perceptions in their favor. They know that thought, emotion, imagination, and belief aren't just nice ideas; they are the levers that move reality itself.

We're all bending all the time, but most of us do it by default, not by design. In the process, we're unconsciously reinforcing the exact outcomes we don't want. We're living in a Reality Cycle we didn't choose *on purpose*. Instead it was built from the momentum of old beliefs, unexamined emotions, and habitual thought patterns that keep us stuck in the same place year after year.

Too many of us live inside stories we never consciously chose. Too many people have stopped imagining what's possible because they've been convinced that "this is just the way it is." Too many leaders unintentionally reinforce cycles that hold their teams and businesses back.

I've seen people bend their reality in the middle of bankruptcy, in the wake of a painful divorce, after a disturbing diagnosis, or standing in the rubble of a business collapse. People who thought they had *nothing* left built lives they wouldn't trade for anything else. And I've watched leaders completely rewrite the culture of companies on the brink of implosion.

Not because they learned some new productivity hack.

Not because they lucked into a perfect set of circumstances.

But because they transformed into Reality Benders. They learned how to interrupt the cycle running their lives, rewire it from the inside out, and aim it toward a vision they actually wanted.

I know this because I've been there. I've drifted through seasons of my own life, going along *with* the flow instead of choosing *where* to flow. I've been knocked flat on my back, facing obstacles I thought I'd never get past. I've stood at the edge of losing everything I'd built and felt the weight of fear so heavy it almost convinced me to give in and give up.

I've also lived on the other side. I've rebuilt from nothing. I've bent reality to match a vision so vivid it felt more real than what was in front of me. And every single time, it came down to this: **The world you live in is being shaped by you whether you mean to shape it or not.**

Let that sink in for a minute. You probably need to go back and reread it. Underline it and put a star next to it. (In fact, there will be more than a few sentences like this in this book that are easy to read quickly but deserve a second look.)

The key to changing your life isn't willpower; it's not about working harder; and it certainly isn't about lucking into a perfect set of circumstances. It's about becoming aware of how you see the world, learning how to interrupt the cycle that's keeping you stuck and rewiring it to point toward the vision you want. And to do that, you must change the unconscious thought and emotional patterns that govern your visible world.

I wrote this book for two reasons:

1. **Personal Transformation**—I want to first help you think differently about your reality. Then I want to give you the practical tools you need to take control of your own life, break the cycles holding you back, and build the future you actually want—not just settle for the one you're reluctantly living.

2. **Impact**—I come alive when I get to help leaders make an impact with those they lead. Leaders have a unique opportunity when they bend reality: They have the chance to improve the reality of others. However, this kind of impact isn't just for capital "L" Leaders. As you'll learn, we all have a sphere of influence and the opportunity to lead. No matter your leadership role, no matter if it comes with a title and a corner office or a clipboard and a crossing guard sign, once you master your own Reality Cycle, you'll have the tools to help others do the same—your team, your organization, your family, your community. The ripple effect is enormous.

Welcome to *Reality Benders*—a guide for people who are ready to become conscious creators instead of unconscious participants. Here's a word of warning, though. This isn't about trying to "think positive," or repeating affirmations in the mirror. It's not about chanting in a dark room for two hours at 5 a.m. This is about mastering the inner architecture of your mind, the power of your emotions, and your imagination to *bend* the trajectory of your life. It's powerful. It's practical. And it's something anyone can do.

Don't worry—we aren't abandoning reality here. We're reimagining the cycle creating it. Your current circumstances are not your destiny—they're just the latest output of an inner system. And systems can be changed. So consider this your invitation to…

- Go beyond circumstance.
- Question "the way it is."
- Imagine without limits—fueled by the best feelings you've ever known.
- Lead without pretending.
- Live with your eyes wide open—*creating* the future, not just surviving it.

When you change your reality, you clear a path for others to change theirs. Let's bend reality—together.

Greg

You are not a finished product; you are a living design.

Restart. Reset. Refocus.

Reality bends for those who refuse to quit the work of becoming.

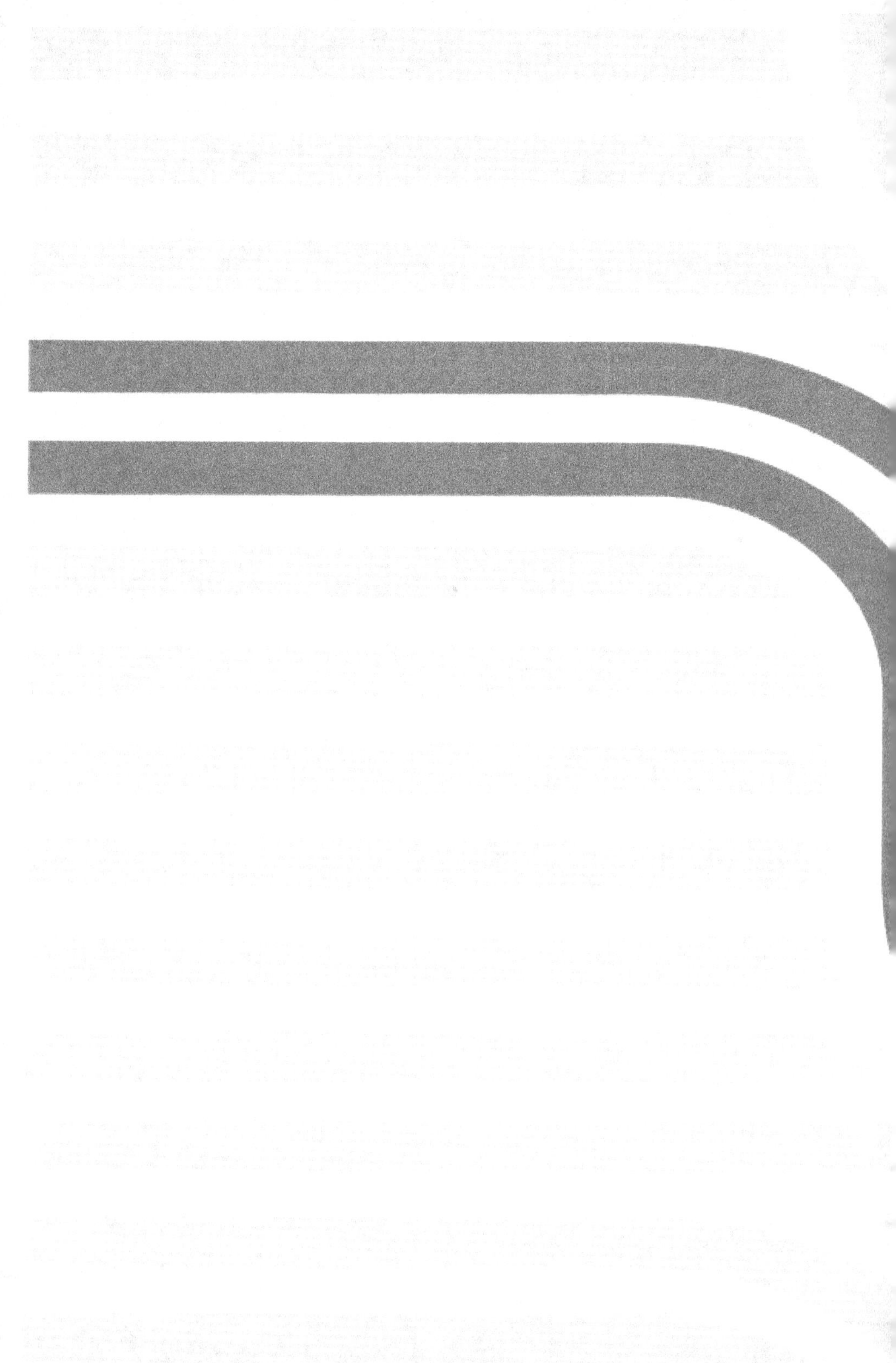

part one

THE STORY OF YOUR LIFE

chapter one

RETHINKING YOUR REALITY CYCLE

whistle blows somewhere behind you. The next thing you know, a red rubber ball the size of your head is flying at your face faster than you can move. Turning your head to avoid a broken nose, the ball feels like a boulder slamming into your cheek and rattling your brain. As if in slow motion, you feel your body falling toward the lacquered wooden planks of the basketball court below you. You instinctively reach out, your arm absorbing the shock, allowing you to control the rest of the drop.

Lying on your side, you watch those around you, most weaving and swerving to avoid attack, a daring few racing for balls to launch at their opponents.

How did I get myself into this? you wonder. *How can I turn this around?*

For most of us, life feels like a game of dodgeball. We focus all of our effort on avoiding a direct hit to the face. And only when a small victory seems guaranteed do we grab the ball and attack. The problem is that when we spend all our time on defense, reacting instead of acting, we lose control of the game. We give up our chance at victory to others brave enough and bold enough to capture a ball and throw it. We throw up our hands and drift through the game—and life—allowing whatever happens to determine our fate, as if we have no power to change it.

But what if you could guarantee your victory? What if you choose to win, no matter the outcome? Would you dive for the ball? Would you take control and throw yourself into the game? Or would you continue waiting, doing your best to avoid all the balls flying at you?

Let me ask a different question: How did you create the life you're living right now? Get really specific—what did you want your life to look like? What did you do? What did you think? Did you get the outcomes you wanted?

No matter if you intentionally made certain moves to build your life or accidentally fell into it, there was a subconscious cycle creating the life you're living right now. That subconscious cycle is your Reality Cycle.

The Reality Cycle is built from the thoughts you think, the actions you take, and the way you interpret the outcomes from those actions. The cycle is just what it sounds like—a series of cause-and-effect pieces and parts that fit together to form your life.

Most of us are not aware of this cycle. We believe our thoughts just happen to us, and we usually act in a way to avoid pain and hardship. We don't see the connection between the pieces and parts, so we do what we can to avoid risk—and, with any kind of luck, live quiet, comfortable lives, even if those lives are not very satisfying or fulfilling.

In accepting this life built out of avoidance instead of from abundance, though, we actively give away our opportunity to do more, to do better, and yes, to positively impact the world around us.

We lose out on a life of intentionality. We miss the chance to build something *remarkable*.

Here's an amazing truth you might never have considered.

In every single moment of your life, in every situation, in every interaction, there are *infinite* possibilities. The thoughts you think will determine the actions you take, narrowing down those infinite possibilities into one specific outcome—and how you interpret that outcome is everything. It creates the world you experience. And that experience will either lead you to take a bold step in a new direction, or a half-hearted shuffle deeper into your comfort zone.

You might not like the direction you're headed. Or everything might be great, and you're wondering if you can take it all further, live bigger, and have more impact on those around you. No matter what you're feeling about your life right now, you can change your Reality Cycle; you just have to discover *how*. That's what this book is all about.

YOUR LENS, YOUR THOUGHTS, YOUR REALITY

You wake up for work and discover that you overslept your alarm. You're already running late and you just opened your eyes. Frustrated with yourself and the world, you hurry through your morning routine and pour a travel mug of coffee to drink in the car while you speed to work.

Twenty minutes later, your body and mind start to relax as you pull into the parking lot because you have just enough time to drop your stuff off at your desk and roll into that always-very-important meeting. You tip back the travel mug one last time to drink up the final sip of coffee. The lid wiggles off the top of the mug, smacking you in the face, that last drop staining your best shirt.

Of course this would happen! you think. *This always happens when I'm running late!*

For a split second, you had a chance to change the whole trajectory of your day. You *almost* turned around your thinking from frustration and lack to "This is going to be okay"—but then the coffee. So now, instead of having a perfectly normal and completely fine day, everything that could go wrong will go wrong because you believe it will all be terrible.

When you fall back into bed after this no good, terrible day, you'll solidify your interpretation of the events with this sentence: *I knew it was going to be a bad day when I woke up late...*

While you sleep, your brain will take the events from your day (events which, in fact, were neutral) and tie them to your interpretation of "bad day," so that in the future, anytime these things happen, such as waking up late, you'll "know" that you are going to have a bad day. And guess what? Without realizing it, *you've created the negative lens shaping the reality* of every day you wake up late as a "bad day."

This "bad day" lens will then write a negative script for every day you wake up, thus trapping those days in realities you'd rather not experience.

But the converse is also true.

You can wake up a little before your alarm, feeling refreshed and ready for the day. You have plenty of time to dress, grab coffee, and arrive at the office a few minutes early, giving yourself time to set up for the always-very-important-meeting, which sets you up to nail your presentation.

After the meeting, your boss comes over to congratulate you and asks if you're going to apply for the promotion the company just opened.

The rest of the day is one of the best you've ever had. Everything just goes right.

What you expect, you often find. And what you believe, you build.

As you lie down to sleep, you think, *Wow! I just knew it was going to be a good day when I woke up early...* solidifying the upbeat lens that will write the extraordinary script for every day you wake up early. (Not to put too fine a point on it, but you also could have been frustrated because you woke up before your alarm and let *that* frustration drive the way you approached your day. Starting to see how this works?)

Not every day is completely great or completely terrible, but these simple examples illustrate the Reality Cycle in action, and by extension, the art of bending—shaping your experience with the meaning you assign it. What you expect, you often find. And what you believe, you build.

You don't experience reality as *it* is; you experience reality as *you* are. Your beliefs, emotions, expectations, and past experiences form the lens that filters and influences your interpretation of the world around you. Your inner state determines the quality of your reality. It can sharpen, blur, or distort that reality.

So when you experience a certain outcome, your lens then interprets whether the outcome is "good" or "bad." This label then reinforces or rewrites your perception of said outcome, and moves you closer to or farther away from whatever vision you might have for your life, if you have a vision at all. As you continue to live the cycle day after day, your thoughts become the foundation of specific beliefs, your actions become embedded behaviors, and the outcomes become the lived experiences that reinforce your beliefs.

You can wake up late once and have a bad day, but as your brain strengthens the association between waking up late and the outcome of a bad day, this thinking transforms into the belief that waking up late *will always* result in a bad day. If you *always* think you'll have a bad day when you wake up late, then every following thought will cause you to act in a way that *will* result in a bad day.

We're not born with lenses; we create them. They start out as one-off interpretations of something we experience. Every time the same thing or something similar happens, it becomes reinforced. Your mind loves a pattern, and it's a master at gathering evidence to support whatever story it's telling. Over time, that evidence becomes the bricks and mortar of the reality you live in and an influence on your mood.

If you look through a "not enough" lens, you'll find proof everywhere:

- There's *never enough* time.
- There are *never enough* resources.
- There's *never enough* talent, money, or connections.

On the contrary, if you look through an "always enough" lens, you'll find:

- There's *always enough* time.
- There are *always enough* resources.
- There's *always enough* talent, money, or connections.

Going back to our Monday morning example, maybe as a kid you almost always experienced negative consequences when you woke up late for school. After all, the time crunch can send a spike of adrenaline through your body, causing you to move too fast and make mistakes. Then again, maybe you almost always had good experiences on the days you woke up early. You could sit and drink your milk while your dad had his coffee, giving you a chance to connect before the day began. Both situations, repeated time after time, year after year, set particular lenses and affect how you think about and experience each type of day.

What about those initial interpretations, though? Why would we call something "good" and something else "bad"? There are many things that affect how we initially interpret outcomes and experiences, but it all begins with our personality. Researchers estimate that 20 to 60 percent of our baseline temperament—our fundamental emotional state—is inherited, influenced by our genes. (Think nature.) If you come from a family of optimists, you're hardwired to spot the silver lining; with complainers, you generally scan for problems. Similar for nurture—if you grew up around optimists, you pick up their habits, and so on. This doesn't perfectly account for every person's temperament, but it does explain the foundation of how our initial lenses are first formed, and how we develop certain interpretation biases.

The good news is that our lens is never fixed. Just because you've always interpreted certain outcomes one way (positive or negative), doesn't mean you must and will always interpret them like that forever. In other words, waking up late doesn't always have to mean you will have a bad day. Researchers are finding that we have the ability to shift our initial emotional hardwiring. By intentionally cultivating positivity through reframing, you can shift your interpretation bias, which, in turn, allows you to mold your lens.

When you change your lens, you can change your thoughts.

UNDERSTANDING THE REALITY CYCLE

Earlier we said that the Reality Cycle is built from your thoughts, actions, and outcomes of those actions. But what actually is it?

The Reality Cycle is the subconscious wiring that creates your everyday experience. Because of how the brain works, which we'll get into more later, there are two layers to the Cycle: a short-term cycle that affects your present and a long-term cycle that creates your life, and ultimately, your reality.

Every day you think specific thoughts that cause you to act in certain ways and that result in corresponding outcomes. These three players—thoughts, actions, outcomes—will always show up for every play, *even* if you're not aware of them.

For example, every morning when you wake up and perform a series of steps to get ready for your day, they may feel automatic, like brushing your hair right after you brush your teeth and choosing a certain outfit. But each of these actions is triggered by a *thought*, whether you consciously realize it or not.

In your brain, neurons are firing that tell your body what to do—reach for the toothpaste, remove the cap, set the cap down, etc. *This shirt makes my eyes pop. These pants are too tight. I never liked that skirt, why did I buy it?* As you think and do each thing, you may or may not have an opinion (an interpretation) about the outcome—*Wow, my hair looks great today!* Or *I should've gotten more sleep last night; look at my face!* (In the next section, we'll talk more about how and why we interpret something the way we do.)

Here's a simple image that shows how this plays out in the short term.

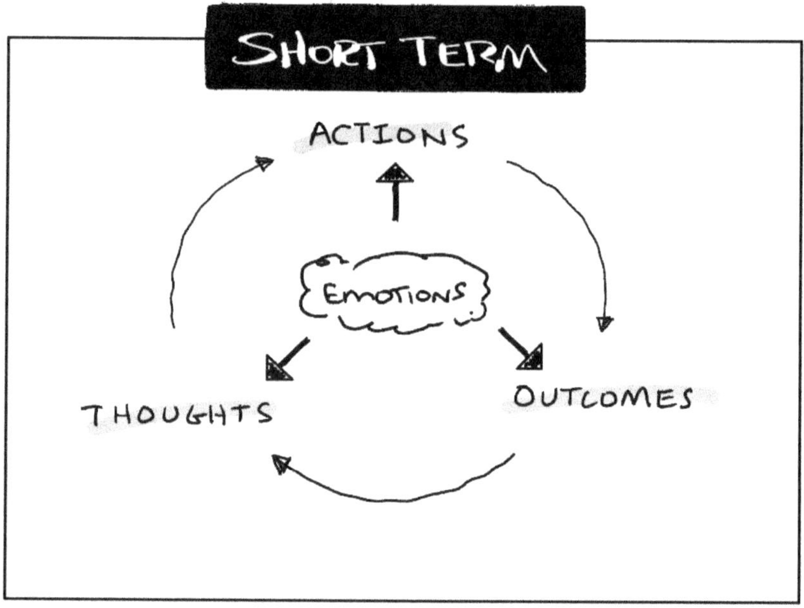

As you continue to move through your day and live out this cycle every second, these thoughts, actions, and interpretation of outcomes build upon each other, subtly shifting how you feel in any given situation. And no surprise here: How you feel, influenced by internal and external events, can affect how you think or how you act or how you interpret outcomes.

The compounding effect of the cycle doesn't stop when you go to sleep, though. Your brain takes the information it collected throughout the day about your thoughts, actions, and outcomes, and moves it from short-term parking to long-term storage. It starts to rewire your brain through something called neuroplasticity. During this conversion process, it also scans for patterns to help it decide the least risky, most comfortable, best-chance-for-survival-way to approach life tomorrow.

It's true: Over time, your thoughts literally change the makeup of your brain.

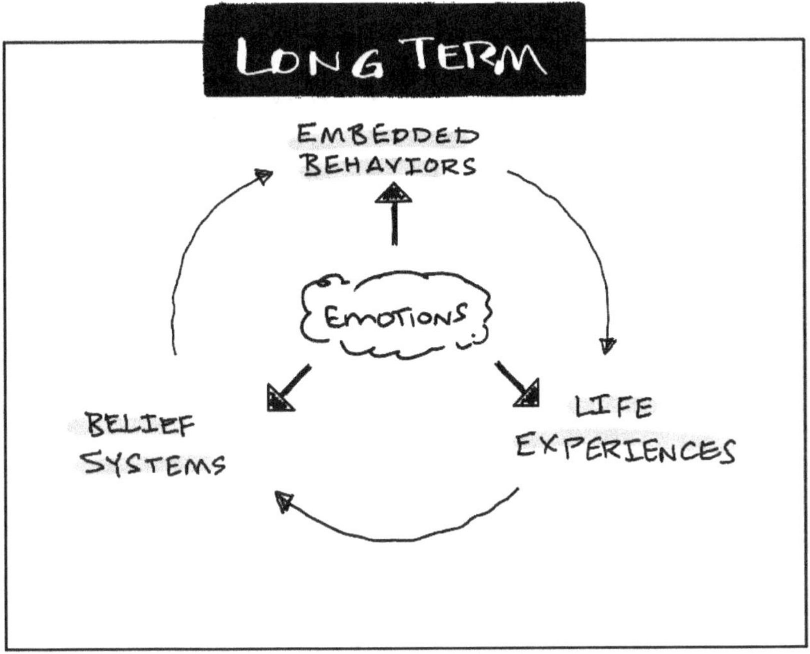

I'm sure you've guessed it by now, but as a result, the longer and more often we think the same certain things and act in the same specific ways and consistently interpret the outcomes, those thoughts transform into our beliefs; those actions become our embedded behaviors; and those outcomes inform our life experiences—thereby establishing our Cycle.

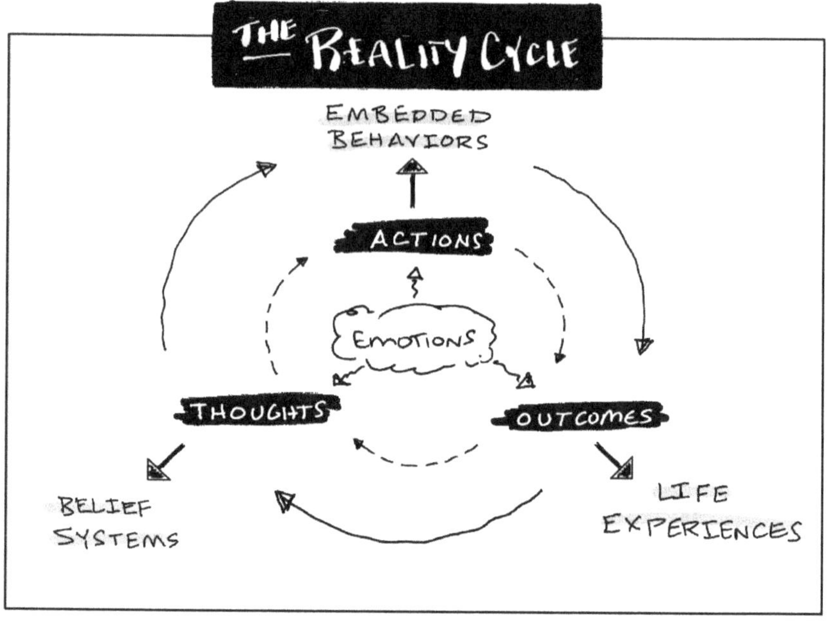

The rest of this book is dedicated to teaching you how to change your cycle by changing the individual parts. So when I say, "bending your reality," or "recreating your cycle," that's what I'm talking about—changing one of the parts to move your life in the direction of your choosing, on purpose.

The more you bend, the more you can change your trajectory at any entry point: thoughts, actions, or outcomes. But for the sake of teaching, I've structured this book to start with how to bend your thoughts, then move into changing your actions and choosing your interpretation of the outcomes.

I don't want to go too deep, too soon, but your imagination and emotion are the key to successfully bending when change becomes hard. Imagination creates the vision of where you're going, and emotion fuels the short-term changes we need to make in order to establish the long-term cycle that recreates our reality.

As illustrated below, they tie this whole process together, weaving short-term and long-term cycles together like an hourglass. As you make changes in the present—one thought, one action, one outcome at a time—each piece of sand siphoning down into the bottom sphere (the future cycle) is a mini-transformation, with imagination and emotion guiding and holding it all together as the glass.

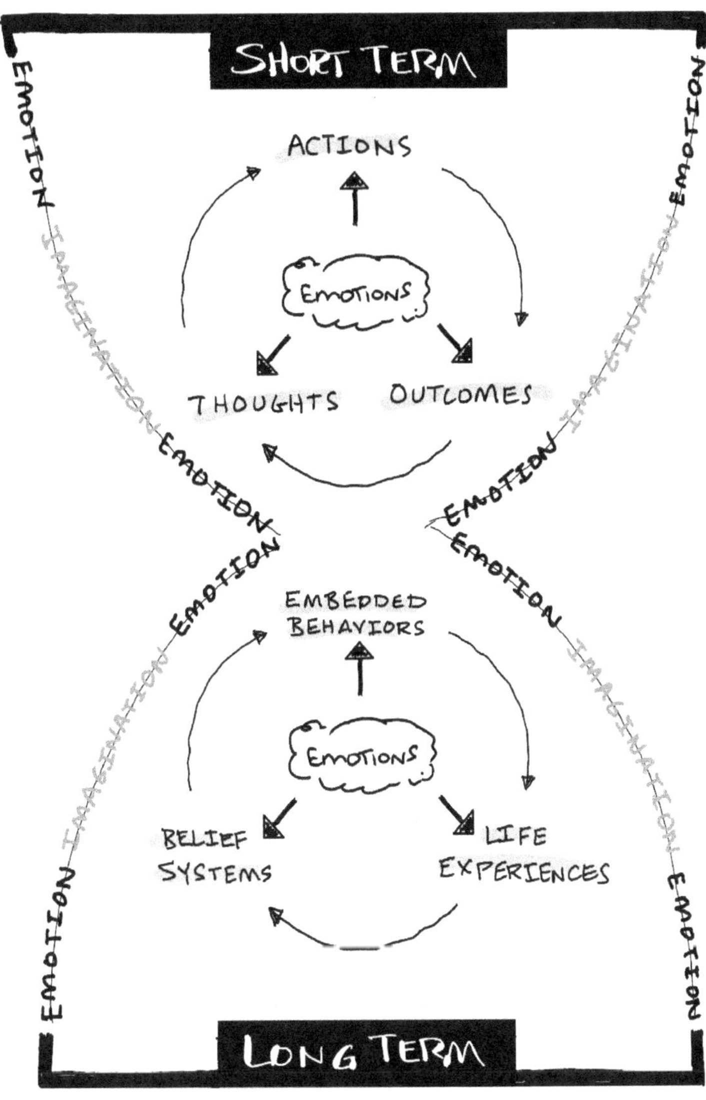

For most of us, all of this happens in our subconscious. We ride the wave of our thoughts, actions, and outcomes because we're not aware of the cycle. Because we're not aware of it, we don't realize we can disrupt it and intentionally choose how we want to think and act in order to get the outcomes we want. Further still, we don't realize we *can* choose how to interpret the very outcomes that build the life we want to live. As a result, a non-Bender's life is often formed without intention.

But that's where hope lives.

Once you become aware of the Reality Cycle creating your life, once you see how the lens (the interpretation and perspective) of your experience shapes your cycle, you can choose how to reinterpret the outcomes and your lived experiences. And in choosing something different, something new, you can bend the cycle to intentionally create a different reality—one you actually want.

THE ENERGY OF YOUR THOUGHTS ON YOUR OUTCOMES, AND THEREFORE, YOUR REALITY

We've all heard the saying, "Doing the same thing over and over and expecting a different result is the definition of insanity." Likewise, *thinking* the same thing over and over and expecting a different outcome is also insanity.

But once you intentionally see outcomes through a new lens, you can shift your thoughts. You can also think new thoughts, which then allow you to reshape your lens. Seeing through a lens of gratitude leads to thoughts of being blessed. Thinking you are blessed leads to a lens of gratitude. However, it also works like this: Seeing through a lens of guilt and shame leads to thoughts of regret; thinking regretful thoughts shapes a lens of guilt and shame.

It's a bit of a chicken-or-egg thing. When it comes to creating a new Reality Cycle, think something new to reform your lens into one of possibility. In turn, you give yourself a different outcome.

While "think a new thought" or even "choose a different thought" seems simple, I don't want you to choose just any old thought. I want you to choose a *higher* thought, an expansive thought, a thought that will begin reshaping your Reality Cycle *in the way you want it.*

We'll talk more about the science of thought in Chapter 6, but for now, it's important to understand that our thoughts are energy in our bodies. However, the energy of your thoughts doesn't stay contained in your body. That energy acts outside of us and around us, too.

If you've heard of the book *The Secret,* or anything about raising your frequency or vibration, you've run into the Laws of the Universe—the twelve or so principles that explore the makings of the universe.[1] Depending on where you look, they may be named slightly differently, but several of them relate directly to the Reality Cycle.

LAW OF MENTALISM	EVERYTHING IS MIND; THE UNIVERSE HAS CONSCIOUSNESS.
LAW OF VIBRATION	EVERYTHING IS ENERGY.
LAW OF ATTRACTION	LIKE ATTRACTS LIKE.

This energy either went out into the world as something positive or became trapped in your body as something negative.

The Law of Mentalism states that everything begins in the mind—our thoughts, our emotions, our unconscious biological processes. Everything. From the mind, as a direct result of the thoughts we have, we either take the actions to make those thoughts a reality or we don't. In one cycle, we apply for our dream job, we start a business, or we sign up for a course on something we've always been interested in. In another cycle, we delete our application, we withdraw our business license application, or we drop out before we've even gone to the first class. The thoughts lead to us taking or not taking actions, which then create a joyful, hopeful outcome or a depressed, I-told-you-so outcome.

But it doesn't stop there. The thought started out as energy in your mind that became the energy of the action or inaction. This energy either went out into the world as something positive or became trapped in your body as something negative. (This is one of those statements I want you to go back and reread—it's that important.) That energy either attracted more of that positive or negative energy into your life because of how it changed your lens.

Don't believe me? Consider the person who continues building and living a life they love even in the face of obstacles or setbacks (positive, can-do lens). Or the master complainer, who is impossibly set back by every little thing that happens to them, and who knows that *every*thing always happens *to* them (negative, can't-do lens). So they never seem to live a life they want or even one that makes them happy.

How do you jump out of the cycle that's not working for you into one that creates the life you actually want?

Raise the energy of your thoughts to reframe your outcomes. **It's the lens—always. Change the lens, change your life.**

A MOMENT AT THE EDGE

I'm a serial entrepreneur by trade. Throughout my career, I've founded and run multiple successful businesses across diverse industries. In 2008, I had built a significant real estate company, scaling heights I never imagined: a portfolio of successful real estate developments, a sense of accomplishment, and the security of family and team. My days were a blur of deals, ambition, and the relentless pursuit of the next big deal. The numbers on the balance sheet went from impressive to staggering. I had banks competing for my business, home builders vying to purchase lots in my developments, and other real estate professionals presenting me with land development opportunities. Every deal I did was a success. I was confident there was no end in sight and the sky was the limit for the business I could build.

Then it happened—the financial crisis of 2008.

The whole country's economic system was collapsing due to an overheated real estate market and out-of-control mortgage loans. Banks were failing and the FDIC was scrambling to shore up the banking system.

Out of nowhere, banks started calling in their loans, demanding repayment, and every path forward seemed to vanish faster than I could chase it down.

Each night, the pressure mounted. My chest felt like a vise. Sleep turned into tossing and staring at the ceiling—wondering if my family would lose everything we'd worked for. Shame crept in where confidence had once lived. I was the leader, the provider, the problem solver—but now I was the problem, unable to stop the tide, unable even to make sense of what tomorrow would look like.

For two years, I fought battles with banks and teams of lawyers looking to take everything I'd worked for. The pressure was overwhelming and relentless. Every day, I went to work knowing nothing good was going to happen. Many of my days began with me getting up, throwing up, and then going to work for a full day of battle. After two years of losing the battles, it became painfully obvious that I was going to lose it all, including the home I lived in.

I remember standing outside my home office, immobilized by fear and failure, realizing I needed to have *the* conversation with my wife. She knew things were bad, but I had shielded her from the worst of it. We were a few months from losing our home and I had to prepare my family for the worst.

How do you look the person who's been your anchor in the eye and admit you've lost it all? That all your belief in yourself, all your drive and hustle, had led here—into chaos, not certainty? I was filled with guilt, defeat, and shame as I stood in the kitchen and began to unpack everything for my wife. The more I talked, the more emotional I became, until I finally reached a point where all I could say was "I'm sorry, I've done all I know to do. I can't fix this. I have no idea what to do next."

There was a silence—a thick, deep quiet that seemed to stretch on forever. In that pause, I felt utterly exposed: my self-worth and self-esteem stripped away, the weight of responsibility almost crushing. I was no longer the man with all the answers—just a broken one, scared and spent.

But then, she turned. Calm, steady, unwavering. She looked at me—not as a burden, not as a disappointment, but as the man she knew, even if I'd forgotten him. "I don't know what to do either, but I know the guy I married, I know who he is, and I'm not worried about it." She spoke these words with a certainty I hadn't felt in months. And then, as if it were the simplest thing on earth, she walked around the island and hugged me. "I'm going to bed," she whispered, and left me standing there in the quiet.

I stood for a long while, stunned. How could she be so calm in the face of what felt like total collapse? How could she see anything worth believing in when I felt like a stranger in my own skin? Yet, in her unwavering trust, she handed me a new lens—one I couldn't find for myself.

Until that moment, I saw only what was lost.

Through her eyes, I glimpsed possibility again.

The next morning, absolutely nothing had changed in the world outside. The magnitude of the crisis remained. But within me, that spark returned—a glimmer of resourcefulness I thought was lost. Her belief in who I was—stubborn, resilient, unbreakable—became the mirror I needed to remember my own belief in myself.

That's what it means to raise the energy of your thoughts. That's what it feels like to change your lens and reframe your outcomes.

Sometimes, we can't see a way through a situation on our own, but someone else's faith can pull us back to ourselves, can help us remember the best in us when we're sure it's all gone. With that best in mind, we can do what's necessary to pull ourselves up and out of one terrible cycle into the one we want. That is *Reality Bending.*

BENDING REALITY AS PROCESS

Bending reality begins with self-discovery. We must first uncover the lens designing our current reality. Once we understand the lens, we can discover what thoughts are shaping our actions and interpreting our outcomes. As we go through this process, inevitably we tap into the emotions fueling the cycle. The next step is dismantling the thoughts holding us back and reforging our lens to guide us in the direction of our vision, of our new cycle.

On the path ahead, you will learn how to:

- Identify and rewrite the Reality Cycle that's been quietly scripting your life.

- Use emotions as energy, not baggage.

- Channel your imagination and vision into measurable transformation.

- Tap into the positive feelings from past successes and bring them into your present as fuel for bold new action.

- Shift from reacting to life to designing it—from the future backward, powered by both memory and possibility.

- Lead others by upgrading the way you think, feel, and lead from the inside out.

Along the way, you'll hear stories of people who bent reality—who shifted the narrative *and* the outcome. People like you, who decided they were done reliving the past and ready to create something new.

Once you unlock these principles and realize your potential as a creator, an even greater adventure awaits: **becoming a catalyst for the transformation of others.** True mastery lies not just in reinventing your own story, but in inspiring and leading those around you—at home, at work, in your community—to challenge their own limits, rewrite their own patterns, and step boldly into possibility.

This book will show you how to move beyond the pursuit of change for yourself and step into your power as a leader—someone who models what's possible, sparks new realities for others, and ignites change that ripples far beyond your own life.

Reality never reaches you unfiltered. You don't experience life as it is.

You experience the life you focus on.

GET OUT OF YOUR OWN WAY

always come back to the story of the farmer and his sons. Determined to prepare his sons for life's unpredictable journey, the father gave them chores and taught them the value of effort. As they grew, a remarkable difference emerged: One son always saw gloom in every situation; the other always found a glimmer of hope regardless of the circumstances thrown at him.

So the father devised a challenge to teach his sons the lessons he thought they needed. He placed a beautiful, gentle pony in one stable in the barn; in the other, nothing but a mountain of manure. The pessimistic son was placed in the stall with the beautiful pony. He immediately began grumbling to himself—even a pony was just an extra hassle that would have to be fed and cared for. The optimistic son was placed in the stall of manure. Knee-deep in the muck, he whistled and smiled as he began digging as if he were searching for something.

The father observed this strange behavior and asked his son, "Why are you so happy?"

He shrugged and responded: "With all this manure, there's got to be a pony in here somewhere!"

This isn't just a parable about attitude. It's a revelation of how your inner narrative—the lens through which you view the world—can transform even the most unlikely scenario into a joy or a burden. Every day, we wake up in a world where the only thing we truly control is how we see it. That lens is the single most underused superpower each of us has because it determines how we interpret, and thus create, the reality we call our lives.

When you're entrenched in this cycle long enough, your thinking evolves into the belief system by which you live your life. Your actions transform into subconscious or naturally occurring behaviors. And your embedded behaviors create the reality you experience—your life experiences—which really shape how you view your world.

To bend our reality, we don't just have to think differently about life. We have to think differently about ourselves and imagine who we want to become.

We don't experience life as it is. We experience it through the lens, the interpretation, of who we believe *we* are. We've spent a lifetime constructing that belief, our self-concept, from the voices of our parents, the expectations of our culture, the judgments of our peers, and the stories we've told ourselves about our successes and failures. The longer our self-image remains the same, the more hardened it becomes within our Reality Cycle.

Once that Reality Cycle takes shape, it becomes self-protecting. Our minds filter reality to defend what we believe. We hold onto the proof that confirms what we already believe and discard anything else that doesn't fit. This is the power of confirmation bias: It preserves our identity, but it can also trap us inside a reality built by reaction rather than imagination.

To bend our reality, we don't just have to think differently about life.

We have to think differently about ourselves and imagine who we want to become.

PERSPECTIVE VS. PERCEPTION: THE STORIES WE TELL OURSELVES

There's a common saying that how you do one thing is how you do everything. I'd take it further: **How you think about one thing shapes how you live everything,** because it affects your perception of the outcome. It's not just what happens that matters, but *how you explain it to yourself—your interpretation created from your perspective.*

Your **perspective** is how you see an event from your point of view.

Your **perception** is the meaning you assign to it and the conclusion you draw from it.

These two, entwined, filter every experience you have, and determine what lens you'll use. Whether or not the optimistic son finds a pony in the manure, he's going to have a great time. Similarly, no matter what would've happened for the pessimistic son, he was always going to have a terrible time. It all comes down to the lens, the interpretation of the outcomes, and the perspective of the viewer.

Science tells us that we're wired for negativity—we remember pain, setbacks, and gaps much more vividly than we do successes. It's a survival instinct. It might be useful in the wild, but it's poison in the workplace, at home, or in your own head. When we evaluate our experiences through a negative lens, we reinforce this negativity bias and create a negative interpretation of current and even future events.

A few years ago, I was working with a research team to determine the best way to help a group of workers improve their performance. Over the past few years, this group had improved a bit, but their competition was grossly outpacing them. So management was trying to determine what they could do to improve performance at a faster rate.

The central part of this process involved meetings where management debriefed the group on their performance in any given activity. They did this in the same way that we usually measure evaluations: They focused on the gaps. They pointed out all the areas that needed improvement, focusing heavily on the most significant gaps.

They would say things like, "You were *this far* from hitting the goal," or "You were this far from the minimum target." In other words, they evaluated performance with a negative lens.

Rather than motivating the team to work harder, though, it increased anxiety in the individual members. They heard those evaluations and thought, *I'm so far from hitting the mark, there's no way I can ever improve enough to make it.* They became overwhelmed by their shortcomings.

It was time for a little science experiment.

To figure out the best way to approach the team, we split the debriefing meetings up into three groups. In one, we didn't change anything. We kept the structure and the language the same. In another, we doubled down on the negativity lens and expressed a sense of urgency for improvement. We even turned up the pressure.

In the last group, though, instead of stating how far from the targets they were, we pointed out where they had improved. We showed how close they were and coached with an attitude of "You're so close, it's just a matter of time."

That little switch made all the difference.

Reframing the evaluation from a negative lens to a positive lens *almost instantly* improved the performance of the third group. They energized, improved, and began to believe success was within their grasp. Why? Because it's easier to think about taking one giant step to reach the finish line than five smaller ones, even if it's the same distance.

Here are some other examples of reframing the lens:

- **Rejection as Redirection:** Rejection is not the end, but a guiding force pointing you toward a better path.

- **Struggles That Shape You:** Consider that your challenges are preparing you for something greater than you can currently imagine.

- **Setbacks as Setups:** Each setback is an integral part of the setup for future success.

- **Life Is Happening *for* You:** Life isn't happening to you, it is happening for you, with every event serving a purpose.

- **Purposeful Delays:** Every delay in your journey has a specific purpose, contributing to your growth and eventual achievement.

- **Failure as a Journey:** Failure isn't a result, it's an event that's a necessary step in your overall journey.

Do you see how you can practically and quickly reframe and create a new lens? What if the stories you're looping in your head are the thing that's holding you back? What if changing just one word in your inner dialogue could open a new path forward? It takes practice, but like any new skill it can be mastered—and quicker than you might think.

WHY DON'T WE CHOOSE TO CHANGE?

Thinking differently begins with intentionality—cultivating the thoughts we want and discarding the thoughts that hold us back, pruning what's no longer in line with our vision for the future so that we can bend our lens accordingly and create a new perspective.

But let's be honest, living intentionally is difficult. If it wasn't, everyone would have this mastered. To choose our thoughts, we have to understand the lens shaping them. And how often do we truly interrogate our motivations? We are not wired to be happy; we're wired to be comfortable.

We're not wired to bend reality; we're wired to make the easy choice.

The gravitational pull to be comfortable and to stick with what's familiar is much greater than the desire to pursue something remarkable. In fact, "comfortable" is an intelligently designed reality cycle of its very own; it can be triggered for many reasons, and often leads to self-sabotage in the face of change. But as Brianna Wiest points out in her book, *The Mountain Is You*, self-sabotage isn't about self-harm—it's often a misplaced form of self-protection.

How might that look in practice? It's going to the same restaurant over and over again because you're too scared to try the new place down the street. At the old restaurant, you know the food will be lukewarm, and the menu will be the same (it hasn't changed in twenty years), but you can rely on this mediocrity.

You want to try a hot meal and something new, but if you go to the new place, what if you can't understand the food because it's too trendy? What if you don't like the way it tastes? What if the portions are too small? Comfortable is safe. Comfortable is still a full stomach, even if it could taste better. You *know* what reality will look like if we choose the old restaurant.

But this book is about pushing your limits, so I have to ask: *What if the new restaurant is so good, it becomes your favorite spot? What if you try something scary and end up liking it? What if this is the start of something exciting?* If a new, more fulfilling meal could be guaranteed if only you expanded your thinking, why wouldn't you open your mind?

Self-protection. That's why.

As you change different parts of your current cycle to bend your reality and ultimately alter your lens, you *will* meet resistance. The outdated way of seeing doesn't want to be replaced. It's literally like wearing a favorite pair of glasses with an old prescription. You like the way they look; that's why they're your favorite. The problem is that you can't see a thing. The words on the page or screen are fuzzy. The images on the TV aren't sharp.

So why don't you go to the eye doctor and update the lenses?

Because it takes time and effort to break free of the gravitational pull of comfort. Intentionality, in other words.

Psychologists have long observed that human beings are wired for consistency. Once we commit to something, especially out loud, we feel a powerful internal pressure to behave in ways that align with that commitment. Robert Cialdini and Melanie Trost called this the Commitment and Consistency Principle.[2]

Imagine verbally committing to buy thirty boxes of Girl Scout cookies. Even if that decision stretches your budget or forces you to borrow money or swipe a credit card, you'll do it because of your verbal commitment. Why? Because backing out would violate the story you've already told yourself and others. You want to be seen as reliable. Supportive. Maybe even a little heroic for buying all those cookies. Your verbal commitment becomes your bond.

This principle does far more than guarantee record-breaking cookie sales. It helps explain why so many of us stay trapped inside the same Reality Cycles even after they stop serving us.

Your lens determines how you see yourself and what feels "normal." Once that lens is established, commitment and consistency silently go to work. When you try to act in a way that conflicts with how you see yourself or how you've always behaved, the conflict can create an intense discomfort. That discomfort has a name: cognitive dissonance. How do we tend to relieve that discomfort? We often retreat. We return to familiar thoughts, familiar behaviors, familiar outcomes.

Not because they're good. But because they're known.

Here's the paradox: The instant you make a true decision, change has already started. A decision sparks movement. It activates one of countless possible futures and begins shaping a new version of you. That shift alters how you think, how you interpret events, and ultimately, how you experience reality.

Reality. Bent.

But to sustain that change, you must be willing to endure the discomfort of inconsistency long enough for a new Reality Cycle to take hold. That requires a new lens.

Your old lens keeps you anchored to familiarity instead of possibility. It clouds your vision so thoroughly that meaningful change feels impossible. When you can't see clearly, you hesitate. And when hesitation sets in, momentum dies.

So you step back. Back into what's comfortable. Back into what you know.

You return to the predictable voice in your head: *I could see this setback as a setup… but for what? Probably failure. So, let's just call it what it is, a setback, and stop trying something different.*

I know this pattern well. I've lived it more times than I care to admit. Over time, I've identified four primary lenses that sabotage change and keep us locked in familiar cycles, sometimes for years: the Resistance Lens, the Limiting Lens, the Change Agent Lens, and the Perfectionist Lens. Don't be surprised if you recognize them in your own life.

The way forward isn't force or willpower. It begins with awareness—seeing the lens for what it truly is: a form of self-protection in the face of uncertainty. And once you can see it clearly, you can begin to challenge it. Later in the book, we'll explore practical strategies for doing exactly that—so you can finally break free from comfort's gravitational pull and bend your reality on purpose.

If you're going to bend your reality, you must stop looking at life through the old, outdated lens. An old lens keeps you trapped in familiarity rather than pursuing the extraordinary. It clouds your vision to the point where you can't make any change because you can't objectively view what's going on.

The Resistance Lens

When seeing through a Resistance Lens, you are comfortable when there are problems to solve or life issues to navigate. In other words, you don't resist battles or life challenges, you embrace them. In fact, you *crave* them. Resistance arises when something is going right, when life is easy. When you start feeling joy, begin to create, or start thriving, you struggle.

Meeting problems head on and initiating change in life is healthy… until it's not. If you are only comfortable in chaos, problems, and constant change, eventually, you will work to create those in your life because you believe them to be a sign of progress, even if others don't.

> ***Reality:*** *When you see reality through the Resistance Lens, you will unconsciously seek out underlying problems because you are most comfortable dealing with chaos or issues that need your attention.*

The Limiting Lens

When you are interpreting life through a Limiting Lens, you subconsciously seek comfort over happiness. (We're not wired for happiness, remember?) In her book *The Big Leap*, Gay Hendricks describes the Upper Limit Problem (ULP) as the unconscious tendency to sabotage happiness and success when you reach a self-imposed limit on how good you're willing to feel (or allow yourself to feel). When you begin to feel happiness that tests your internal limits, you unconsciously sabotage yourself to return to your lower level of happiness because that's your comfort zone.

> ***Reality:*** *If you have a Limiting Lens, it will create a ceiling that impedes your happiness and growth to a level you believe you deserve, which is always less than the one you actually deserve.*

The Change Agent Lens

If you are not only comfortable with change, but you also view it as the primary means of growth and thriving, you have a Change Agent Lens. Like the Resistance Lens, change is good until it becomes a way of diverting attention from the real problem. In this case, going deeper, allowing yourself to develop, or actually finishing what you start.

With a Change Agent Lens, the desire to constantly pivot almost always stems from a growth mindset, but also a mindset of incapability. In other words, you desire to grow in areas of your life that are new for you because you don't believe you are fully capable of becoming what you set out to be. In the end, you are constantly in a state of "fresh start." You are always starting or improving but never finishing. The Change Agent Lens seeks constant reestablishment or reinvention.

> **Reality:** *Experiencing life through the Change Agent Lens will keep you focused on a constant journey of improvement, for better or worse. You will never arrive; you'll always be on the lookout for new and different.*

The Perfectionist Lens

The Perfectionist Lens creates delay driven by fear of failure. Someone with this interpretation is limiting and self-defeating in their pursuit of the flawless conditions needed for their action. You constantly delay what truly matters most, putting a hold on life as you overplan, overprepare, and hesitate instead of moving forward. Your mind becomes consumed with what could go wrong, scrutinizing every detail and imagining the worst-case scenarios. As a result, ambition is overshadowed by self-doubt, and opportunity becomes a source of anxiety. Even small setbacks create a sense of inadequacy and disappointment.

> **Reality:** *Your Perfectionist Lens will keep you stuck, constantly second-guessing, and never feeling quite ready to take the next step (or really any step).*

Whatever lens tends to hijack your perspective, at some point, you either have to accept it (and the Reality Cycle it brings) or decide you're going to change. (Don't skip past this too quickly—a lot of the coaching I do is to help people identify these lenses and decide to see things in a new way so they can create the life they want.)

We all unconsciously prefer familiarity rather than growth, but eventually we become bored and restless when we don't evolve. You can be sure that we'll also be committed to the boredom and restlessness and consistently choose it over change every time. It's the great contradiction in the human spirit.

Reality Bending requires us to resist the gravitational pull of that comfort in order to break free. It requires us to see with imagination and innovation. When you discover which lens is clouding your vision, you can devise strategies to shift your perspective, update your perception, and eventually bend your reality. And it all begins in your mind.

CHANGING YOUR MIND ABOUT YOU

By nature, I always saw setbacks as opportunities. I could always figure out a solution to my problems, and a pile of manure—no matter how big and stinky it was—was no match for me. I almost always had a sunny day—until the crisis of 2008, that is. Practically overnight, my usually sunny interpretation bias morphed from positive to negative, throwing me into a downward spiral. Every time something happened, I reinforced this increasing dismal cycle of thinking with "Of course this happened. And it'll just get worse." When it would get worse, I'd pat myself on the back and say, "I knew it…"

Can you see how easy it is to get hijacked by the old perspective and interpret an outcome with an outdated perception?

When the stakes are high, emotions go higher, and that can lead to some dark places.

But that malleability is what makes the Reality Cycle so extraordinary. One minute, you can be in the lowest state of your life, and the next, with one new and different thought, you can be at your highest, most optimistic self. You just need a reality check to break your current cycle long enough to think a different thought. (This is when you start living intentionally.)

We'll talk about this more in the coming chapters, but on the worst night of my life, my wife was the disrupter (or external catalyst) I needed to think something new. Her confidence stopped my lens hijacking just long enough to give me the chance to question myself. *Why was I going down this path?* It wasn't doing me any favors and it was distracting me from finding a better solution.

Sometimes, to stop that freefall into expired cycles, we need to see ourselves through someone else's point of view, someone else's lens. Sometimes all it takes is a second for your mind to stop, question, and recalculate a behavior in order to think a new thought to create a better outcome, an outcome you actually want. And sometimes, we just need a spark of imagination to see who we can become.

CHANGE YOUR LENS, CHANGE YOUR LIFE

Our entire lives are created in the mind. If you want a different reality, if you want to experience the world in a more positive and powerful way, you must first be aware of this cycle and the way in which your interpretation of the outcomes affect your lens. This awareness is key to understanding the Reality Cycle in a way that allows us to influence it differently.

Change your thinking, change your reality.

At the beginning of this chapter, I told the story about the farmer and his sons, but in that story, the father failed to change their minds. He failed because he was going about the transformation in the wrong way. He thought it was enough to put them into favorable or unfavorable circumstances and naturally, they would move toward a more flexible attitude. But simply changing someone's environment isn't enough to change the way they interpret the world. It can help, but there is more that needs to be done. After all, if you move to a new environment, it may be new, but without intentionality, you're still the same old you, an unchanging constant in the equation.

The farmer needed to show his sons how they were viewing the situation, bring awareness to their thought processes, and, from that awareness, show them how to consciously choose to *stop* a certain thought in its tracks or *start* thinking in a certain way. He needed to help paint a new version of their lives and help them imagine how life could be, not how it was.

As we talked about in Chapter 1, there are infinite versions of you based on the specific lens you use (ie., how you see yourself and the situation—a concept we'll keep exploring), the choices you make, and the behaviors you build. What you think in this moment will determine your actions, and in turn, which version of you that you become, and so on. Every choice you make and action you take determines the next set of choices. It's the branching decision tree of the endless possibilities that create your life.

For example, you could

- Keep reading and learn how to change your reality into something better.
- Put this book down and listen to a podcast that leads to a new idea.
- Ask that person for a date and possibly meet your future spouse.
- Decide to finally stand up for yourself and speak up.
- Quit the job and start your own business.
- Send the email and ask for a raise.
- Sell the house and buy an RV.
- Start an exercise habit.
- Eat another Oreo.
- Take a nap.
- Laugh.

Each of these are choices with consequences and outcomes. Some are big, some are small—all are unique and set off a chain reaction of future decisions and outcomes. But with so many choices available, how do you decide which one to make? How do you decide when to say yes and when to say no?

Look to your imagined vision for the future for direction.

Let's say Future You wants to sell your house and travel around the country in an RV in six months. That means Present You needs to do several things:

- Find a realtor
- Research RVs
- Fix up the house

- Locate and buy said RV
- Learn how to care for the RV
- Create the skeleton of an itinerary (at the very least)

There are more things we could add to the list, but this is a good start.

As Present You is planning and acting in accordance with Future You's desired cycle, your boss calls you into the corner office.

"We'd like to offer you a promotion with a significant raise, an additional week of vacation, and five more shares of company stock," she says.

This is a situation you'd never considered. Even though you hate your job, maybe more money and benefits would make it easier to accept? You could still buy the RV and take it out for a week or two at a time if you had these additional vacation hours.

What do you do?

You look to your imagined vision for guidance.

On one hand, how will Future You who isn't in an RV but still works for The Company in a higher position with more stress, *feel* in six months? Does Future You regret saying yes? Is Future You overworked and tired? Is Future You actually taking time off to travel?

On the other hand, how does Future You driving through the mountains, parking at a campsite in Yosemite National Park, hiking and photographing wildlife feel? Are you fulfilling your childhood dream of visiting every national park? Are you picking up your nieces and nephews for short trips to places they've never been? Are you creating memories that will fundamentally make your life better?

Who do you want to be in six months?

It is possible to change the way you experience the world. It is possible to create whatever life you desire. However, it doesn't start with changing your job, house, or car. It begins with deciding who you want to be and how you want to be.

I know which cycle the Reality Bender You would choose. Do you?

It is possible to change the way you experience the world. It is possible to create whatever life you desire. However, it doesn't start with changing your job, house, or car.

It begins with deciding *who you want to be* and *how you want to be.*

Here's your invitation: First, challenge your default interpretation. You can't always control what happens, but you always control how you narrate it. Second, imagine who and how you want to be. Let that vision guide your thoughts and actions. When you shift your thinking to align your perception with your desired outcomes, that's when you can change your reality.

Everything changes when you realize you are not merely at the mercy of events—you're the author of them.

If circumstances can shape emotion, then emotion can shape circumstance. Reality Benders don't wait for circumstances to change their emotions—they use emotion to change circumstances.

chapter three

RECREATING YOUR CYCLE

ack in the early 1980s, a young man stepped onto an elevator in Atlanta, Georgia, headed up to the office for work. There was nothing remarkable about this situation—people use elevators all the time. But in the 80s, people couldn't stand in silence watching cat videos on their phones. So that young man struck up a conversation with the older gentleman next to him.

This older gentleman had a huge problem he was trying to solve: He was trying to get the news out about a business he owned, but no one would take his advertisements. His business was considered taboo, and it was the last thing anyone wanted to be associated with. He'd been all over town talking with the best ad agencies about how to get radio air time, and none of them could do it.

That's when the young man spoke up.

"I'll do it," he said. "I'll get your business on the radio and anywhere else you want it."

Now this young man had no idea what he was talking about. He didn't own an advertising agency. He'd never worked in advertising. He didn't even know the first thing about putting a campaign pitch together. But he was aware of what he didn't know, and he knew he could figure it out or find the right people to help him. He just needed a chance.

The older gentleman liked his enthusiasm and told him to come by and give him a pitch.

As soon as the young man got off the elevator and into his office, he slammed the door and started calling up everyone he knew to see who could help him land this deal. Two of his friends who were between ad jobs stepped in and together, the three of them landed the deal.

Now they had to make good on their promises.

Because of the nature of the business, these young men had to be enterprising. If they got a "No," they couldn't stop; they had to figure out how to pivot, how to get the "Yes." They could see success in their minds' eyes, so they worked backwards step by step to determine the actions they needed to take to make it happen.

After months of hard work, more "No's" than they'd heard in their entire lives, and even more ingenuity—they did. They created an ad campaign that not only got on the radio and billboards and in local magazines, but they won an award for how good it was. And in the process, they formed a new ad agency that went on to be wildly successful for many years.

That young man was me.

And that's the story of my life—I told you I was a serial entrepreneur—as a young man, I didn't always know what I didn't know and sometimes I did understand how much I had to learn, but that naïveté always gave me the courage I needed to make (mostly) anything succeed. It allowed me the freedom to imagine any kind of future I wanted and the ingenuity to figure out what I needed to do to make that future come true.

Until a few years ago, I didn't know what the Reality Cycle was or that I had been bending it to my advantage for most of my life. What I said in the Introduction is worth repeating here: I wrote this book because I want you to understand how the Reality Cycle works in your life and what you need to do to bend it to your advantage.

I want Reality Bending to become second nature to you, your default setting.

In Chapter 1, we discussed the steps in the Reality Cycle and how our lenses are formed. In Chapter 2, we focused on the pitfalls of getting caught up in old stories and becoming waylaid in a Reality Cycle that doesn't work anymore. Before we begin to reconstruct your Reality Cycle, there's one last element to discuss: the role of emotions. *Feeling more of what you want to feel is the energy that fuels your efforts and bends your reality.* (Go back and read that one again. Maybe even underline it so you don't forget it. It's that important.)

Feeling more of what you want to feel is the energy that fuels your efforts and bends your reality.

EMOTIONS: THE DRIVERS OF THE REALITY CYCLE

When I started recognizing and mapping out the Reality Cycle, it was easy to see how actions led to outcomes. You do one thing and another happens. Cause and effect. Make sense? Even still, it wasn't hard to realize that we take action based on what we're thinking. (Don't believe me? *Hmm. I wonder what's happening on your social media feed right now? Any chance there's a new update you missed?* If you're tempted to put this book down and pull out your phone to check right now, *that* shows the power of thoughts.)

Understanding that thoughts precede actions was one thing; finding the key to how and why we think certain things was a tougher puzzle to solve.

Our thoughts are usually either subconscious and sending out commands that keep our lungs breathing, our hearts beating, or our instincts guiding us, or they're a response to a stimulus. You walk into a room, see someone you recently argued with, and suddenly, you can feel your muscles spike with adrenaline, your heart beating faster, and the heat rise in your face. You're emotionally reliving the argument. Because of this emotional trigger, you might imagine what it would be like to walk over and speak to that person, and so on. The thought initiated the emotion, which led to subsequent thoughts, then actions and outcomes.

Yet this process could just as easily originate from an emotion. If you're still carrying around the anger and resentment from the argument, even if you're not dealing with your adversary, your thoughts will be tinged with this aggression and come out in ways you might later regret. After the confrontation, maybe you stop by a coffee shop, order a drink, and it comes out wrong. This reignites the fire simmering just below the surface, and you're rude to the overworked barista, who then profusely apologizes for the mistake and makes you a new coffee. She didn't deserve your negativity, but the emotional state of your mind set you up to be hostile.

Another outcome might be that the barista snapped back, and suddenly you're in another conflict. And so the cycle continues.

As you learn more about how you interact with your Reality Cycle, you'll see that you can initiate bending at any point in it. But for the sake of creating a clear, step-by-step way into the process, we'll focus on our emotional state because emotions and beliefs are the anchors of the Reality Cycle.

When we are mired in emotions that keep us down, on edge, or ready for a fight, our realities will reflect this back to us. It's the Law of Attraction in motion, "like attracts like." If you want to change your Reality Cycle, examine what emotions have been driving you. They may have started out as hope or joy, but as our cycles get going and we fall into outdated ways of seeing, those emotions are transformed. That's when comfort and fear of change seep in. But here's the most insidious part: it's such a gradual change, we don't usually see it happening.

The young man from the beginning of the chapter could've had a perfectly good life in advertising. He was enthusiastic, up for a challenge, and right at the start of his advertising career, he did something no one else could do. But he's stuck in a Change Agent Cycle. His inherent nature thrives on the new. If he'd stayed around too long, he would've become bored and bitter, and his once shiny and desirable Reality would've become scuffed and tarnished to him. He would've moved from eager to live to eager to retire.

Instead of transforming into this muted version of himself, though, he noticed when his feelings about this particular Reality Cycle shifted. These feelings were hints that it was time to create a new cycle. Sometimes they were little annoyances at hiccups in the process—someone forgot to call the printer about an ad, the radio host misread the advertising copy, the coffee pot was empty when he went to pour a third cup. But he intrinsically understood what they meant. And so he knew that it was time to imagine and create a new Reality Cycle.

When you begin the process of changing your Reality Cycle, it's uncomfortable. It takes intentionality to upgrade your thinking. It requires courage to act in a new way. It calls for an open mind to reinterpret outcomes. But that's how you create a different lens and break free from a Reality Cycle that no longer serves you.

RELEASING WHAT'S NO LONGER WORKING

I once knew a man who was a smoker. He'd smoked a pack a day for a long time. A few times over the years, he'd considered quitting, but it never lasted long. Maybe he could go a few days without a cigarette, but inevitably, he'd have a stressful work day or he'd find himself in a social situation where he typically smoked (and where other people would be smoking), and he'd give in.

Just one, he'd think. But one would always turn into two, and he'd buy a pack at the gas station on the way home. After failing so many times to permanently quit smoking, he decided it didn't really matter to him. He truly didn't care if he smoked or not, and he actually kind of liked it, so he decided to give up on giving it up.

A few years after throwing in this towel, he and his wife had their first baby, a girl. He loved holding his daughter and rocking her to sleep. At his daughter's first birthday party, his wife wanted to take a picture of him holding the baby. He'd just lit a fresh cigarette, though. So he put the cigarette in his right hand and held the baby with his left. But then he saw it—the baby started wiggling and swatting her arms around to get the smoke out of her face. She even cried a little. And that did it.

The father looked at the baby and looked at the cigarette, and you could see the pain and emotional conflict in his face. Just as quickly, resolve replaced the pain and conflict. He decided right there that his daughter's comfort and health was more important than that cigarette. He put it out, threw away the rest of the pack, and I never saw him smoke ever again. It was quite remarkable.

When I asked him how he had been able to go cold turkey, he said that every time he had a craving or thought about lighting up, he remembered what it felt like to see the discomfort on his daughter's face. He'd tap into the *emotional pain* he'd felt at the memory of her swatting the smoke. The emotion influenced him to understand that's all the craving was—a momentary thought. And that was it. Once he had this understanding, the craving was gone, along with the idea of smoking.

What you feel consistently does not stay internal. It spills outward into decisions, behaviors, and outcomes. What you feel repeatedly becomes what you practice. What you practice becomes what you create.

If you have a goal in your life, you can certainly work to achieve that goal. But commitment and continued effort are emotionally driven. Behavior is emotionally driven—emotion is the engine. It gives thought momentum. It fuels imagination. It reinforces belief and determines whether action happens or stalls. What you feel consistently does not stay internal. It spills outward into decisions, behaviors, and outcomes. What you feel repeatedly becomes what you practice. What you practice becomes what you create. So if you want to keep achieving your goal over and over, or if this goal is part of a larger process, you have to cultivate the right emotion; you have to tap into emotional attachment.

Emotions connect to the motivation for a behavior, and as we've mentioned, a behavior is a sustained action that over time becomes an automatic response. But I didn't completely understand that connection until about six or seven years ago through my coaching with business leaders.

It doesn't matter who it is or what the situation might be— leaders always have some frustration because they're leading other people. Leading in and of itself always contains an aspect of trying to affect change in people's lives. Leaders are either trying to steer people towards being part of something bigger than themselves, which is this organization and the organization's mission, or towards being part of a team and contributing.

So years ago, I started noticing that leaders were constantly frustrated because they would identify a behavior they didn't want in someone they led, and they immediately addressed the behavior to try to change it. But it never worked.

I started asking them, "Have you ever thought to ask what's *driving* the behavior?"

Usually that was met with a blank stare. You could almost see the wheels turning in their minds. *Well, no, Greg, because I just need them to change their behavior.* That's when I understood this key point: You're not going to change a behavior that's rooted in a belief system *or* a thought process; you have to change that belief system, and in turn, the thought process follows. And to do that, you have to get to the heart of the belief system, the emotional core.

You're not going to change a behavior that's rooted in a belief system or a thought process; you have to change that belief system, and in turn, the thought process follows.

When these leaders started asking the question, or investigating to find the why behind the what, and started working on that mindset or thought process, *that's* when they had breakthroughs.

So what's the lesson here for you?

When you can find the *right emotion* to fuel this process, you can *sustain the action* you want to *achieve the outcome* you desire, over and over again. In other words, you crack the code on living with intention.

HARNESSING THE POWER OF INTERNAL AND EXTERNAL CATALYSTS

Some people can wake up one morning and decide they're going to change, so they do. But most of us need a wake-up call. The wake-up call can be either a catalyst from within (internal) or a catalyst from the outside (external). An external catalyst usually comes in the form of an event or another person, like that baby girl swatting away the smoke and causing my friend to put his cigarettes down for good. The swatting away of the smoke is an outcome of smoking; the emotion that my friend felt watching his child was the internal catalyst he used to stay committed to quitting.

Think of internal catalysts as a strong emotion created from an undesirable (or desirable) outcome. That emotion starts a new mindset, and the combination of the mindset and the emotion begins the new reality cycle. We want to teach people to cultivate emotions and mindsets from their successes as much as we want them to from disappointments.

Both internal and external catalysts bring the need for change to our attention, and once we're awake to the need, we can begin to cultivate the right internal environment to sustain us through the transformation when it gets hard, and we're tempted to fall back into old patterns. This becomes the emotional anchor tying us to our new Reality Cycle, spurring us on when all we want to do is have one more cigarette.

In the coming chapters, we'll go through the process of imagining a new Reality Cycle (think of it like creating the roadmap to get to your desired future) and how to create the emotional anchor as your internal catalyst to keep you going throughout the process. But before we move on, I want to get to the heart of why you're ready to bend your reality and the catalyst that made you realize it was time for a new Reality Cycle.

Reflection is an important part of bending reality. Especially the first time, or even the first few times, until this becomes a natural and unconscious process in your life (a constant internal catalyst independent of the external), I'll encourage you to take moments of mindful reflection to keep reminding yourself why you wanted to bend your reality. In fact, we're going to do this again in Chapter 5 with an exercise I call "Mining the Past." But for now, begin thinking about your catalyst and your why.

When I was thirteen years old, I was a rotten kid. I was always in trouble and because of that, I was ostracized. Parents didn't want their kids spending time with me. I never got invited to birthday parties. I never went to a sleepover or had good friends. I was headed down a pretty dismal path.

Most of my life, people told me, "You're a waste. You're good for nothing."

So I wasn't surprised when a voice over the school's loudspeaker called me down to the principal's office. At the time, our principal was a great man I really looked up to. On this particular day, I figured I'd get another round of detention and the usual talk, but instead, I was devastated by his words.

"Greg," he said, "there are people in this world who are just rotten apples. They're worthless and they infect everything they touch."

I just sat in front of his desk, quietly listening to this new speech. He went on. "You need to understand that's who you are.

You're a rotten apple. Why don't you just quit school? You don't want to be here, and we don't want you."

I had absolutely no idea what to say. I'd heard versions of this all the time, but never from someone I admired. Maybe he was trying reverse psychology or something else, but instead of encouraging me to try better, my whole demeanor sank.

If he thinks I'm completely worthless and hopeless, what's the point?

He waved me out of the office, and I dragged my feet down the hallway back to my science class. I slunk back to my seat and kept my eyes on the floor for the rest of the period—not that I'd been paying attention anyway.

The bell rang, and over the noise of my classmates gathering their books and leaving, my science teacher, Jane Moring, called out, "Greg Cagle, I need you to stay a few minutes over."

Oh great, another lecture, I thought. I didn't know what I'd done to deserve this one, so I took my time picking up my books and walking up to the science table at the front of the class.

"Young man, I could not let this day go by without telling you that I don't see you the way others see you," she said. She spoke with such an urgency in her voice that she must've known or suspected that I wasn't thinking anything good.

"There's something unique about you," she went on. "I see a really special young man. I've watched the other kids around, and I just know there's something special about you."

I almost didn't register what she was saying. It certainly wasn't what I expected. I glanced up at her face to double check that she was talking to me, and then quickly looked back down at the Bunsen Burner on the table.

"I think you might even be a leader. I don't know what it is, but if you'll let me, you and I will discover what that special thing is."

She stopped talking and waited for me to respond. I could feel the weight of the anger, the resentment, the disappointment, the hurt, everything that had been filling up my heart, suddenly drop. And absence of that emotion gave me room to breathe a little. I could feel tears filling up my eyes, but I was a tough, thirteen-year-old kid; I wasn't going to cry in front of my teacher, but gosh, I couldn't express to her what her words meant or what they did for me in that moment.

So I shook my head yes, and said, "Yes, ma'am." And left as soon as I could.

From that day forward, this wonderful woman coached me, mentored me, encouraged me, and advocated for me like no one had before. She stuck by my side all the way from eighth grade through high school, where I stood on the stage, graduating second in my class. She sat in the front row, cheering me on.

If you went back and asked that thirteen-year-old Greg, "Are you going to run your own business someday? Are you going to write a few books? Do you think you'll be a keynote speaker on a stage teaching audiences about leadership, team building, and communication?" he would respond, "No. I think you've got me mixed up with someone else."

But if it hadn't been for Jane Moring being an *external catalyst* waking me up to the need for change and then helping me through that change every step of the way, I honestly don't know if I'd be here right now.

That's the power of an external catalyst.

It won't always take such a strong external catalyst to wake you up. Once you've bent your reality a few times, your internal catalyst, the one that senses the need for change, will be there to guide you. Either way, the power of a catalyst jump-starts the process by shifting our belief system (especially our beliefs about ourselves and what's possible), rewarding behaviors that encourage us to act differently, and helping us view outcomes more positively than negatively.

So I'm going to ask again, *why* are you ready to bend your reality?

Don't just rush through this. Sit in it for a while.

What or who woke you up to the need for change?

Think about it, write it down, hold onto it. (Seriously, go ahead. I'll wait for you.)

We all have a lens that filters how we see ourselves and others. And our lens can keep us trapped in a Reality Cycle that no longer works for us. So when someone or something wakes us up to that fact—when a loved one or a coach or a situation makes us realize that it's time to do something new, that we can do something different, that we have the power of choice—we need to hold onto their words. We can borrow their hope for us, we can dare to see differently, and we can begin to bend our reality one thought at a time, one act at a time, one interpretation at a time, over and over again, until we see the world through a new lens.

Now let's get bending.

The most powerful version of you is not discovered; it is created, born in imagination, strengthened by thought, and proven through action.

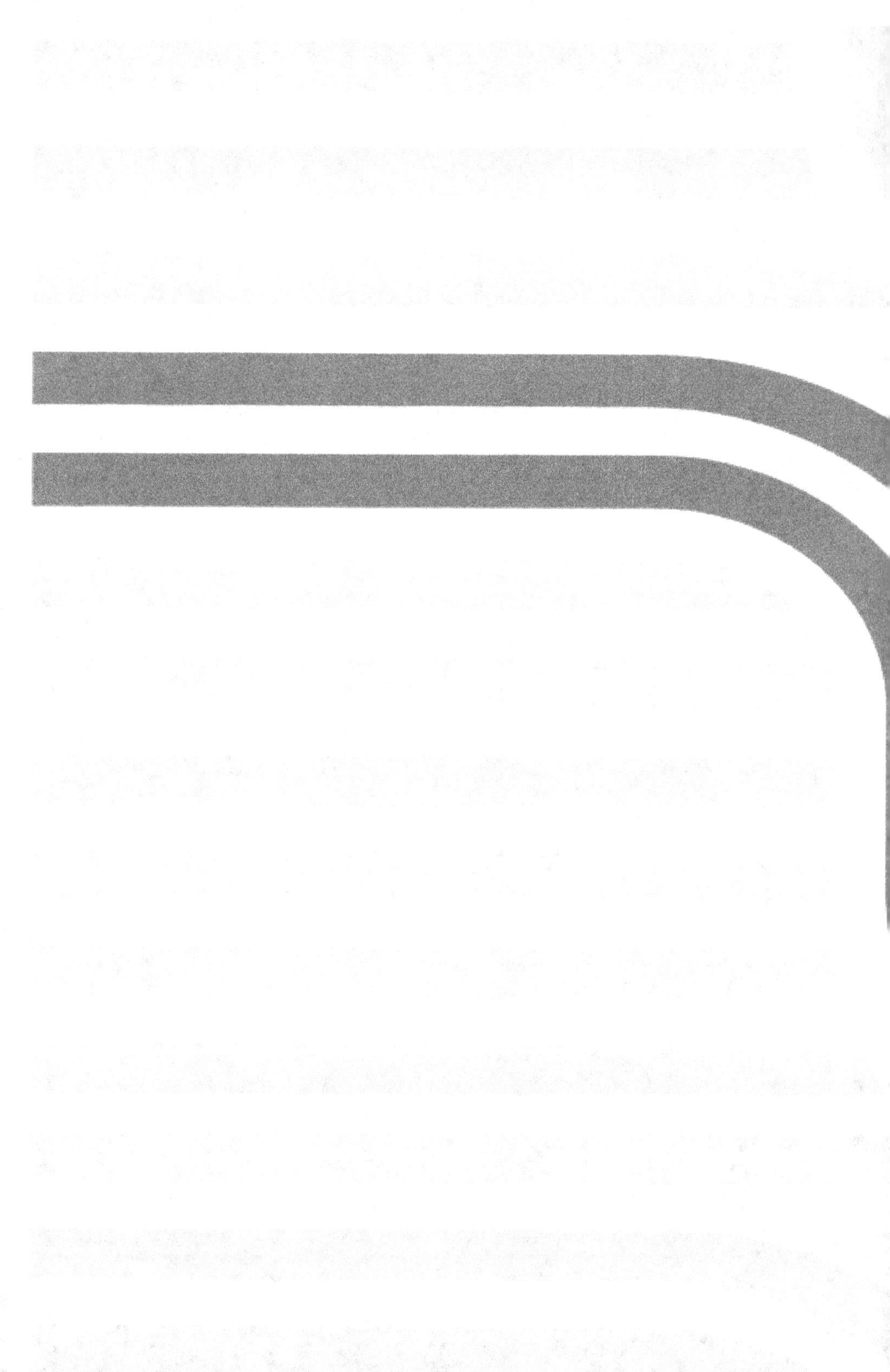

part two

THIS IS HOW YOU BEND IT

chapter four

REIGNITE YOUR IMAGINATION

n 1961, President John F. Kennedy captured the imagination of a nation with his famous Moon Speech. He gave us a seemingly impossible goal that, if achieved, would launch us into a new version of the future—one with spaceships, aliens, and Jetsons-style living. It was magical. It was expansive. It was exactly the kind of vision we needed to help us focus on something hopeful. We were excited to push the limits of what humankind could do.

He didn't shy away from the fact that it would be *hard*. He leaned into it:

> We choose to go to the Moon in this decade and do the other things, not because they are easy, but because they are hard; because that goal will serve to organize and measure the best of our energies and skills, because that challenge is one that we are willing to accept, one we are unwilling to postpone, and one we intend to win, and the others, too.[3]

While we imagined speeding off into space in sleek, shiny rockets, our minds free from the constraints of reality to dream and imagine anything and everything, the scientists and engineers cursed and chain-smoked in windowless work rooms, trying to figure out how to make this wild vision a reality.

There were three main ideas about how to get a man on the moon. The first two, direct ascent and Earth-orbit rendezvous, were based on concepts and designs already in use. Theoretically, starting from what we knew worked and just making it bigger and stronger could work in the long run.

But we had less than nine years. There wasn't time to improve these plans enough to get us on the moon.

The third option, lunar-orbit rendezvous, would require the existing Saturn V rocket and two smaller vehicles, and that was it. The catch? Once the Saturn V rocket launched everything into space, those two smaller vehicles—the command module and the actual lunar landing vehicle—would have to meet up and dock *while moving in space.*

No one had ever done that before.

The risk was unbelievable, and most of the NASA team did not want to do it. Yet the biggest proponent of this idea, an engineer named Dr. John Houboult, believed it was the only option to make the president's (and now the nation's) vision come to life.

No one could've anticipated the outrage Dr. Houboult received. Many saw him as an outsider, as he wasn't considered part of the core decision-making team. They didn't like his pushback against their ideas nor his tenacity to put his theories forward. They told him he didn't know what he was talking about, that his math was bad, and that he was out of his lane, essentially.

Collectively, they *knew* too much. (We'll dive into this a bit later.)

They *knew* everything that could go wrong (and some of which did). They *knew* what they couldn't do based on physics, mathematics, mechanics, and the limits of existing resources. They *knew* what others had tried before that had ended in failure. Their knowledge and experience trapped them, and almost convinced them that landing on the moon just wasn't possible.

But Dr. Houboult's outsider status did two things for him: First, it gave him the freedom to imagine something new—he wasn't tied to the old way of thinking. Second, it allowed him to *see* and *seek* solutions where others saw only problems. He felt so strongly about lunar-orbit rendezvous that he risked his career and reputation by circumventing his superiors to directly address the highest echelons of NASA leadership, who eventually listened.

After months of fighting, the right people finally saw the value in Dr. Houboult's proposal and agreed with him. Their minds had been opened just enough to see his vision for landing on the moon and could imagine how it might be possible.

Finally, on July 20, 1969, when Neil Armstrong took one step for mankind, Wernher von Braun, one of Dr. Houboult's initial adversaries-turned-ally and chief architect of the Saturn V rocket, told Houboult that he'd had a really good idea.

I love this story because for all of human history, walking on the moon was impossible—until it wasn't. Everything is impossible until someone does it. Nothing exists until someone envisions it and brings that vision to life.

When I look back on all the stupid successes of my life, I never should've achieved a single one. But I did because I had enough imagination (the vehicle) to see the vision (the finish line) and figure out how to get there. Think about the story at the beginning of Chapter 3—who did I think I was, telling a business owner that I could get his untouchable business on the radio, and later on billboards and in print ads? I had no idea how to do those things, but I had the *vision* of doing them and I had the *imagination* to figure out how to get them done.

In its most simple form, to bend your reality, you must first *envision a different future* and then *engage your imagination* to get there.

ACCEPTING THE CHALLENGE OF IMAGINATION

When was the last time you used your imagination? Earlier today? Earlier in the week? Ten years ago?

We usually associate the word *imagination* with children playing pretend games, but adults use their imaginations all the time—*you* use your imagination all the time; you may just not remember that's what you're doing.

It's not complicated: Imagination is literally the act of making something up in your mind.

That's it.

Every time you go over a conversation in your head, saying that thing you actually wanted to say (rather than what you said) and playing through the scenario, you're imagining. Every time you daydream during a meeting, you're imagining. Every time you plan a vacation, seeing and feeling how relaxed you'll be versus how tense you are right now, you're imagining.

We allow ourselves to freely imagine things all the time—so why do we hold ourselves back from imagining a new Reality Cycle?

Because we're stuck living present-forward instead of future-back.

As adults, we get trapped in the details of daily living, especially if we have families. It's a constant rush of waking, making breakfast, getting everyone where they need to be, working all day, getting everyone home or shuffled off to various activities, cooking dinner, and going to sleep, with a thousand other minute tasks and thoughts draining our creativity and energy. If we can find a moment to ourselves, we're thinking about the next immediate step in the day or trying to plan for X, Y, or Z. We don't allow our minds the space to dream and play. And if we do have the time for such frivolities, who has the energy? We could create the vision of a different reality, but really, would we be able to actually make it happen? Probably not, so why waste the energy? Why get our hopes up?

That's present-forward living: It's reactionary. It's making decisions from a scarcity mindset. It's seeing all of the problems with getting to the moon because *we know too much* about how gravity and mechanics and the way the world works. But when we do this, we cut ourselves off from all of the other possible Reality Cycles we *could* be living and get stuck in the narrative of now.

To walk on the moon, to create the life we want, to do something that (as of now) is impossible, we need to be a Reality Bender; we need to live future-back. Future-back is just like it sounds—we imagine the future we want, tap into the emotions that evokes, and then instead of starting where we are and convincing ourselves we'll never get there, we stand in that amazing future, assume it's a done deal, and start moving forward like it's already a reality.

To continue the moon story, we need to imagine the Reality Cycle where we break through the atmosphere, emerge into space, and bounce out of the lunar lander onto solid ground, and determine what changes we need to make to become that version of ourselves. Future-back living is *pulling* Present You into the future, not trying to *push* Present You right now.

You may not want to walk on the moon—that's fine. It's a stand-in for any new Reality Cycle. Maybe you want to be a world-renowned speaker or a Fortune 50 business executive or an international jet-setter or own a bakery that sells the best cupcakes in the state. Whatever your desired reality is, that Reality Cycle begins in your imagination.

It is an extension of who you are right now, an expansive— you might say *imagined*—version of you. (You think those Apollo astronauts didn't spend time *imagining* how cool they would look in those space suits with their mission patches on their shoulders?)

When kids imagine life as adults, some of them stick to what they know (firefighter, doctor, dog-walker) and others let their imaginations run wild. They envision a highly exciting, not-always-realistic life (ballerina-ninja-cowgirl, anyone?) What ends up keeping most of us from pursuing those uninhibited dreams is the daily tedium of life we mentioned earlier, but experience and knowledge also gets in the way. As we grow, we pick up experiences and knowledge that mold and shrink our ideas about what is possible.

This isn't necessarily a bad thing. Knowledge and experience help us focus and take life one step at a time. They allow us to learn the skills we need to live. As we age, we're eventually paid for our knowledge and experience. The more of both you have, the bigger your paycheck, ideally. However, rather than guiding the journey always onward, eventually knowledge and experience become the very roadblocks keeping us from doing more, from changing, from getting to the moon, from becoming Reality Benders. We often make this trade-off subconsciously, without understanding what we're losing.

At some point, we turn down the volume of our imagination. We pivot from wanting to act on Broadway to creating role-play training scenarios while working in HR during the day. We paint our artwork in the garage at night after the kids have gone to bed and then hang it in the living room instead of the Louvre. And that's okay, right? Or do knowledge and experience whisper that it must be okay because only a fraction of aspiring artists make it to Broadway or art museums? That it's practically impossible to make a good living in those realities?

The more you know, the more rigid you get about what's possible and what's impossible.

Yet what if you could reinvigorate your imagination and live a new reality based on who you could be rather than who you are now? Who you are right now is only one version of you. And, by the way, if your heart is still beating, it's not the finished product. For most of us, the version of ourselves today is a smaller version of who we could be because we've experienced and learned just enough to know that we can't, shouldn't, or don't deserve to grow beyond our current selves.

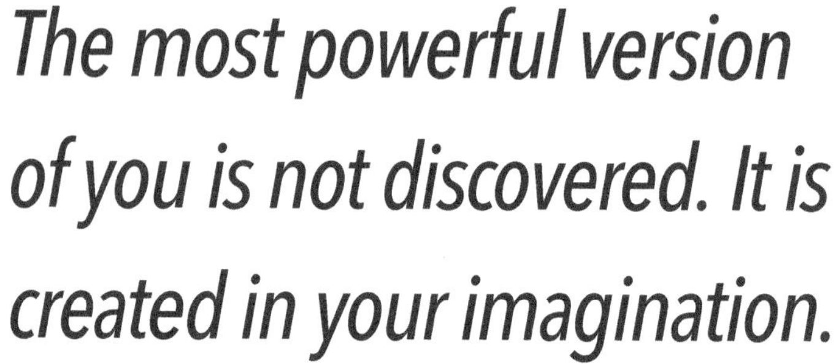

It's time to let all of that go.

You may not be named an NFL MVP, but you could absolutely build a strong speaking career, traveling around the country and world giving presentations based on what you've learned as a business owner for the past ten years. Rather than allowing your knowledge and experience to limit your future, leverage it to create a new vision for the future, and use your imagination to figure out how to get there.

The most powerful version of you is not discovered. It is created in your imagination.

That as-yet-uncreated version of you does not arrive through clarity or confidence. It arrives through imagination—long before there is evidence.

Remember this: Imagination is not fantasy. It is a rehearsal. It is preparation. It is the quiet act of seeing yourself beyond your current identity—before your behavior has caught up, before your environment confirms it, before anyone else believes it's possible.

ASPIRATIONS VERSUS ABSOLUTES

A couple of years ago, I was sitting in business class, flying to a meeting. Thousands of people do this every day. I was and am a business man. I've done this work for so long, it's become part of who I am, how I define myself, and believe myself to be.

About halfway through the flight, I looked around the plane and saw a woman across the aisle reading a book—which is remarkable, because so many people read digital books these days. Curious, I glanced at the cover to see what she was reading. It was *The Four Dimensions of Culture*, the book I'd written and published earlier that year! My face was printed on the back cover. I couldn't believe it.

By that point in my career, I'd written and published two books—*The Four Dimensions of Culture* and *Be Weird*. Some people, like my wonderful wife, called me an author. But I didn't see myself as an author or a writer. I was a businessman who had some ideas about how to do business better. I'd never encountered someone reading something I'd written. Sure, people would comment on social media posts and people even wrote reviews of my books, but here, right next to me, was proof—a stranger who found enough value in what I had to say that she traded hard-earned dollars for my words. It blew me away. It was an external catalyst that started to shift my thinking about myself.

I wasn't just someone who wrote books; I was an actual author, and she proved it.

I couldn't help but smile. I wanted to know what she thought about it, but I didn't want to stare at her the whole time trying to gauge her interest.

Eventually, the seatbelt sign turned on as the plane prepared to land, and I couldn't help myself.

"What do you think about that book?" I asked her, giving her a nice three-quarter turn like my author picture.

"Oh, it's really good," she responded. I waited for her to notice that her right hand covered my face on the back, and asked her a few more questions.

You can't change your Reality Cycle until you give yourself permission to imagine a seemingly impossible new life.

She didn't catch on.

The plane landed, and the other passengers started shuffling down the aisles with their luggage.

"I hear the author's a great guy," I said, pointing to the back of the book as I stood up with my briefcase.

She flipped it over to look at the picture. Her face crinkled as she processed what I was saying and who was on the cover.

I smiled and waved at her as I left. I have no idea what happened after that, but it wouldn't have mattered. My mind had shifted and my imagination had grown during that short flight.

I'd become the author I'd always wanted to be. Reality Bent.

CREATING YOUR REALITY-BENDING ROADMAP

You'll never change your Reality Cycle if you don't open up your imagination to what it could be—and it can be whatever you imagine. There are infinite possibilities for your life. What do you want it to be right now?

I couldn't be an author until I allowed myself to be one. It's the mindset shift from *I have some things I'd like to write about* to *I am an author.* You can't change your Reality Cycle until you give yourself permission to imagine a seemingly impossible new life. I want you to think about all the obstacles, all the impossibilities, and then set yourself free from them. Unburden yourself from what you think is possible or impossible. Stop thinking about what you know. Quit this limited version of you and your Reality Cycle.

Grab a pen or pencil and a piece of paper. Right now.

Set this book down for a second. You can come back to it later.

Now allow yourself to think about the new Reality you want for a minute.

- What does it look like?
- What are you doing in that Reality?
- How is your thinking different?
- What different beliefs do you hold to?
- How differently are you acting in this new Reality?

As you imagine your new Reality, write down all the things you'd need to do or become in order to live it. Do you need a new business permit? Do you need to take any classes? Do you need a food truck? Take a few minutes to list everything. I'll wait.

This is a list of the barriers and obstacles you need to overcome in order to create your new Reality. How's it feel looking at this list? Overwhelming? Impossible?

What are you going to do about that? QUIT THAT MINDSET!

Crumple up that paper and throw it in the trash. Really. Trash the paper. We're physically breaking the knowledge and experience holding you back from pursuing your new Reality.

As you move forward into your new Reality, there will be points when your knowledge and experience will try to convince you that what you're doing is impossible, that it won't work, and that you'll have to revert to your current Reality Cycle that's keeping you right where you are today. Don't listen to it. When that happens, write out everything that feels like a barrier, then crumple it up. Burn it. Do whatever you want to destroy the obstacles so you can get back to imagining the next right step.

In 1989, Tony Robbins challenged me to imagine a new reality, and it started with a van. Back then, Tony Robbins was growing in popularity, hosting seminars and selling his popular series on cassette tapes. One of the exercises he asked listeners to do was write down in detail the kind of car they wanted. Every single detail you could imagine.

So sitting at the kitchen table, I scribbled out everything I could imagine about the customized conversion van I wanted to buy. (Don't laugh, it was the 80s. Those vans were rad.) I knew I wanted to take my family on trips, so I wanted the seats to fold down into beds where the kids could rest. I wanted a small TV mounted on the inside, captain-style chairs that could swivel, interior lighting running down both sides of the seating, and on and on, all the way down to the color of the van (steel gray with a blue stripe).

As I wrote down these details, all the reasons why I hadn't purchased one (all the barriers to that Reality), swam through my head: *They're expensive, they're not practical for daily living, we don't have the garage space for one…*

But the more I imagined this van, the stronger my desire for it grew. I started getting ideas about how I could bring one home, and those ideas grew louder and louder as well. By the time I finished the exercise, the obstacles keeping me from this van had weakened. They had been transformed from absolutes I could never overcome into faint whispers, until they eventually disappeared.

About three years later, I was cleaning out my office, and I found this van list in an old journal. Smiling, I was reading through my description when it hit me—that *exact* van was sitting in my driveway. It was the same color and everything. After I'd imagined the van, I'd continued with Tony's tapes, journaling about a new exercise every day. As the tapes went on, this listing had become buried until I'd forgotten all about it. And yet, between then and my office cleaning, I'd done it—I'd created the Reality Cycle I needed and I bought the custom van for my wife. The transformation had taken place without me even realizing it.

That same transformation is happening to you right now, even if you don't realize it.

In Chapter 2, we talked about why people don't change, the biggest reason being that they don't see the results they expect. The manifestation of change hasn't happened yet, so they don't think anything is different, but it is. That change is occurring at the deepest level: our belief system, which affects our thoughts, our actions, and our outcomes.

Right now, you are on the verge of a new Reality Cycle. You know what it looks like, but to make it happen, you need to know every detail about it. You need to get curious about this new life. You want to set the vision of where you're going. You must *see* yourself in your new Reality before you can *be* there. When you know what the vision is, every single thing about it, then you can imagine how to get there.

When I was young, right out of school, I had a roommate. If you walked into his bathroom, you'd see a picture of a Porsche cut out from a magazine right in the center of his mirror. But that's not all. This guy went so far as to cut a picture of his head out of a photo and paste it on the person's body driving the Porsche so it looked like he was driving it.

This Porsche was the first thing he saw in the morning. Whenever he brushed his teeth, shaved his face, anytime he went into the bathroom, it was right there. Every day, he would say, "I'm this guy," and point to the photo. "I drive Porsches. I wear Rolexes. That's who I am." The great thing? He went on to great success. He worked hard and created the Reality Cycle where he *was* that guy, and he still drives Porsches and wears Rolexes.

Living future-back, creating the roadmap to your new Reality Cycle begins by saying, "Who is that version of me? Who do I need to be in order to be the person living that Reality Cycle? How would I walk? How would I talk? What would I focus on in that reality?"

There are infinite possibilities for your life right now.

Pick one. Don't worry if it's the "right" one—there is no "right" one, just the one you want right now. Focus on those details—that's your next Reality Cycle.

Next, we'll create the emotional fuel to get you there.

You cannot bend reality while clinging to yesterday's habits.

Eliminate what anchors you to the past—and step forward as someone new.

chapter five
EMOTIONS, ENERGY

n 1946, a baby girl was born in a small log cabin in Tennessee. She already had three older siblings, and eight more would follow her. The girl's family was poor but happy. Her ancestors came from Wales to the New World and brought with them the old songs and stories, which her mother shared with her children. As this girl grew, it was clear she had a gift—she always had a song in her heart that she wanted to share with the world.

And the world loved it. They couldn't get enough of her.

This girl grew up singing in the Pentecostal church her granddaddy led. They didn't have much, but they had love and they had God. Years later, as an adult, she would recount the moment that changed her life: An older woman in the church approached her, dabbed her forehead with oil, and told her that she was anointed. She was destined to do great things.[4]

That moment ignited the passion that continues to drive her every day. Her faith in God and her belief in the calling He gave her became the well she returned to every time life in the music industry was tough—and you can only imagine how difficult it was for her to break into a male-dominated business and be taken seriously as a woman and a performer. But as she famously says, she stayed true to herself and her values, and just kept going. Even in the darkest depression, when she wanted to quit everything, she turned to her faith in God and found the strength to overcome.[5]

From a log cabin in Appalachia to becoming the most famous woman in country music to an award-winning philanthropist for her work in children's literacy, Dolly Parton relied on her faith to sustain and propel her through the heartache and hard times to unimaginable success.

To be a Reality Bender, you will have to cultivate resilience in the face of setbacks—and the strongest and most resilient anchor is emotion. You will have to find the emotional fuel to carry you from your current reality to your new reality. Everyone who has ever bent their reality knows it. For some, that emotional anchor is a positive experience that changed them or touched them at the deepest levels, such as a faith encounter; for others, it's the tough, character-building moments they vow to never forget or suffer through again. No matter what that emotional anchor is, it's crucial for developing the internal catalyst to push you through the pains of bending your reality.

You may already have a deep, emotional anchor that's helped you get to where you are right now. Or you may be someone who shies away from the sometimes-intense self-work required to find that emotional anchor. Whatever the case may be, your future success and your ability to bend your reality hinges on emotions.

For a long time, people believed that rational thought was the primary driver of intelligent decisions and that emotions were merely distractions. But modern neuroscience has revealed that reason and emotion are interconnected systems—the front and back of the same coin. Thought provides logic, while emotion gives those thoughts meaning and energy.

Separating one from the other weakens both.

Without emotion, goals lose urgency and decisions lose direction.

Rational thought allows us to interpret data, but emotion tells us *which* data matters. Without emotion, goals lose urgency and decisions lose direction. As neuroscientist Antonio Damasio introduced in his 1994 book, *Descartes' Error: Emotion, Reason, and the Human Brain*, when emotion is impaired, even logical decisions collapse. People can analyze forever but feel no clear preference, because nothing *feels* significant. Emotions, then, are not barriers to performance; they are the very signals that help us prioritize what we value and why we act at all.

Emotion doesn't derail logic—it directs it.

It fuels perseverance, giving purpose to persistence when the results seem invisible. Harnessing emotion, rather than suppressing it, creates the energy we must have to bend reality.

CHANGE IS HARD BUT NOT IMPOSSIBLE WITH THE RIGHT EMOTIONAL FUEL

Change is hard for two reasons, which we touched on in Chapter 2: it takes time, and we're wired for comfort. Those are your biggest obstacles when it comes to bending your reality.

At this point, you've created the vision of where you want to go. You are beginning to see how the Reality Cycle can get you there. But your life won't change overnight. It will take consistent action *and consistent emotion* over time to recreate your life on the outside and to transform yourself on the inside into a self-perpetuating Reality Bender.

Right now, I'm going to ask you to move toward your vision without any meaningful manifestation of it. The manifestation (or the outcome) of change is always delayed. That's just part of the deal. And the more you're bending your reality, the bigger the change you want to make, the longer that change is going to take to actually manifest itself. But in the absence of a manifestation today, tomorrow, or next week, without achieving our desired outcome within even a month, it becomes difficult for most people to keep going, to keep doing the work that's making the new reality possible.

Here's a concrete example that will resonate. Every January, people flock to health clubs to start working out, lose weight, and "get healthy." Maybe you've been one of them. You may even have a vision of what you want: *I'm going to lose ten pounds. I'm going to fit into my skinny jeans. I'm going to take off my shirt at the beach without being embarrassed.* So you diligently wake up every morning before work, make the trek through the dark to the glowing, cement building full of equipment, put in your time on the treadmill or with the weights, and journey back home, tired yet proud. Then, after seven days of this, you step on the scale, just knowing that something had to have changed by now. After all, you've worked hard every morning.

But instead of a lower number, you discover that you've gained two pounds.

That one moment of defeat can stamp out your vision of a new reality in seconds because the manifestation you expected did not appear despite all the effort you feel like you've put in. You ask yourself, "Does hard work actually pay off? Is this current discomfort of doing something different actually going to be worth it?"

Yes, it will be. But you have to keep going.

You have to sustain the effort without the evidence of manifestation, at least for now.

Every meaningful transformation will eventually be met with resistance, fatigue, or self-doubt. In those moments, emotion becomes the differentiator between those who persist and those who give up. Rational goals shape the direction, but emotion creates and preserves the momentum.

And that's the hard part. We're so conditioned to getting everything, instantly, that things that take time (and everything worthwhile in life takes time) that we give up far too soon.

What the scale can't tell you is the invisible work that's happening inside you. You're slowing down the buildup of cholesterol in your heart; you're increasing your aerobic capacity; you're strengthening your joints; and you're rebuilding forgotten muscles (which, by the way, can account for those extra two pounds on the scale.)

The change is happening in ways your choice of measure can't gauge.

But it *is* occurring. You just need to have faith in the process. This is a big deal—not everything that is happening can be seen. And not to put too fine a point on it, but often the most important things—faith, love, confidence, loyalty, courage, instinct—*aren't* seen, at least not directly or immediately.

Our reality is grounded in three things: our beliefs, our behaviors, and our experiences. If we're going to bend our reality, we have to get at and change our ingrained belief system that's been there for a while. And it doesn't want to leave very easily. That's the second reason change can be hard.

This ingrained belief system doesn't want to go away. It likes being there, and we like it there whether we admit it or not, because we know it and we're comfortable with it. Remember the lens traps in Chapter 2? Remember that our minds are wired for comfort and familiarity over anything else? We want success, but we want to find it down the road of familiarity. Well, unfortunately, what we want requires entering the waters of unfamiliarity.

When we're taking the steps to do something different and bring about a new reality and we're not seeing the results, we become frustrated. That frustration, the disappointment, the negative feelings that may arise are part of that old belief system reemerging. It's trying to convince us that the change we want will never happen. It's the voice in your head saying, "I told you so—working out is for schmucks. You're never going to lose weight. Why don't you just go back to that warm, comfy bed…"

While change is certainly hard, it's not impossible.

There are people in the world bending their realities all the time. And you can join them. You can become a Reality Bender, but to get through this initial problem with inertia, you must dig down deep and find the reason, *the emotional fuel,* the motivation for the change.

Every meaningful transformation will eventually be met with resistance, fatigue, or self-doubt. In those moments, emotion becomes the differentiator between those who persist and those who give up. Rational goals shape the direction, but emotion creates and preserves the momentum.

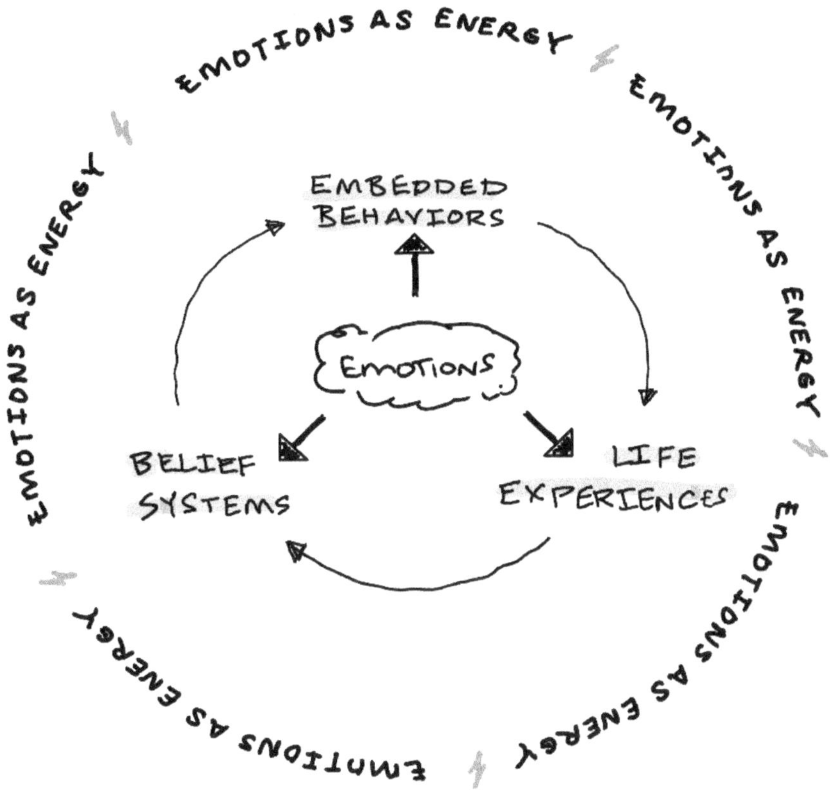

Think of emotion as the energy currency for long-term transformation. Vision paints the picture, but emotional engagement keeps the brush moving. When properly understood, emotion is not random; it's data—data about what we value, what we fear, and what we must protect or achieve. Reality Benders know how to engage their emotions, and they don't just think about the path forward—they *feel* their way forward. That's the kind of emotional alignment that makes change sustainable and embeds those behaviors, life experiences, and belief systems that create a new reality.

Vision gives you the destination. Imagination keeps you excited. Emotion fuels the actions and discipline necessary to stay the course.

Vision gives you the destination. Imagination keeps you excited. Emotion fuels the actions and discipline necessary to stay the course. At some point you will want to quit. To keep moving forward, you need an emotional anchor that you can return to every time and use it to keep yourself moving forward.

Most successful people have a story to tell, and it's often one of overcoming adversity. They all have stories like having the electricity cut off three times a month because their family couldn't pay the bills or having a parent who worked three jobs to pay the rent. They were latchkey kids. Those experiences built the behaviors and beliefs necessary to get away from those tough beginnings. In these cases, the negative emotions of growing up in hard environments created the emotional fuel necessary to break free from the cycle of poverty. It kept them going, doing the hard things, outworking everyone else, in order to create the lives they wanted or to avoid the life they experienced in the past.

You can't use just anything as emotional fuel. The struggle is breaking free of the constraints of the comfort that keeps pulling us back, the reemerging old belief systems. So the emotional fuel must be foundational—it must be strong enough for us to break the gravitational force of our comfort.

This doesn't mean we're simply repeating positive affirmations to keep us going (though you may use them at some point, and you'll find some great Reality Bending statements at the end of the book). This doesn't mean we're berating ourselves for having negative thoughts on tough days (which you might have at some point). It does mean we dig deep, we become acutely aware of *why* we do *what* we do, and consciously choose the best new *Why* for the new *What* that we want.

Do that, and you become your own internal catalyst. Do that, and you will bend your reality any way you want. But it starts with using your emotional fuel to shift the behaviors long enough to get the experiences you need to move your belief system in the direction you want to go.

REALITY BENDING RUNS ON EMOTIONAL FUEL

In the current version of my work, I spend most of my time coaching clients one-on-one and leading group presentations and training sessions. For one of these sessions, I was conducting a John Maxwell exercise with a group of C-suite clients to help them uncover which of their values to use as decision-making filters.

It was sometime after lunch, and the leftovers of our sandwiches had piled up in the center of the large, oval table dominating the conference room. I walked around and gave each person a deck of cards; each card listed one value—things like gratitude, respect, trust, loyalty, honesty, and so on.

I asked them to go through the cards and pull out their top five values in life. Because values inform and influence our decisions, I wanted to help them understand their motivations. Afterward, I began asking them which cards they had chosen and why. Simple yet powerful. To kick off the sharing, I turned to the CFO, a man named Carl, and asked him to name his number one value.

This particular group of people had worked together for years and knew each other very well, which isn't always the case. And Carl didn't hesitate to deliver the punchline we all knew was coming: "Money," he said.

Everybody in the room started laughing.

"Oh yeah, that's Carl," someone said.

Another person added, "He's all about that money. He still has the first dollar he ever made."

When the laughter died down, I asked another question. I knew there was something deeper going on here. There always is.

"Carl, help us understand. Why is money your number one value?"

Carl looked down at the "money" card in his hand, quiet for a second. Then set it down on the table and lifted his eyes to the room.

"When I was a kid," he said, "there was a particular time that came around every year. And every year, I got tied up in knots, full of anxiety, just dreading it. The closer that time came, the more anxious I became. In fact, one year, my whole body broke out in hives because I was so upset and stressed."

Carl stopped talking, and no one said anything. They watched him intently. For all they knew about each other, this was apparently something he hadn't shared with them.

"That time of year was heading back to school," Carl said. "I *hated* the first few weeks of school. When it was time to go back to school, all the parents would take their kids to buy new school clothes, new school shoes, new backpacks, everything. And I always got my cousin's hand-me-downs.

"I would show up to school with scuffed shoes, the soles already worn thin. My shirts were threadbare, and my 'new' jeans were torn, my knees starting to show through the fabric. Then it would start."

By that point, you could hear a pin drop. I don't know about the other people in the room, but I could feel the dread Carl talked about in the pit of my stomach. I remembered being that kid with the hand-me-downs, the clothes that had already seen better days before I had a chance to leave my mark on them.

"The other kids would bully me to the ends of the earth over my clothes," Carl continued. "Most of the time it would end after a few weeks, once another kid had brought attention to themselves over something stupid, so the bullies would forget about me. But everything changed in seventh grade.

"All the kids were at recess on the playground, and one of these bullies beat me up because of the shoes I wore. No one stood up for me. The others just stood around and watched—glad it wasn't them, probably. It was humiliating.

"As this kid finished and stood up, he jeered at me and laughed. 'Where'd you get those shoes … Patches?' And that did it.

"The nickname 'Patches' stuck. From that time one, no one knew me as Carl; everybody called me 'Patches.'

"You want to know why money's my number one value? Because my three daughters will *never* go to school in their cousins' clothes."

I think about this story a lot. It's a clear example of how emotional fuel drives sustainable effort and change.

At some point in Carl's life, he had to make a decision—how hard was he going to work to change his situation? How long was he willing to work hard without seeing the results he wanted? His answer: as long as it took so that his future kids, should he have them, wouldn't have to go to school in their cousins' clothes.

But Carl's story illustrates more than personal grit; it shows how emotion and belief interlock to guide decisions. His childhood pain didn't just create motivation—it gave meaning to his adult choices. That emotional charge reshaped not only *how* he worked but *why* he worked the way he did. It placed a high value on money not for wealth purposes but for love of family.

Motivation itself is emotional; it's a blend of desire, fear, and hope driving purposeful movement toward a goal.

This aligns with what psychology and neuroscience confirm: We cannot think or decide without emotion. Motivation itself is emotional; it's a blend of desire, fear, and hope driving purposeful movement toward a goal. Frustration signals motivational misalignment. Gratitude strengthens courageous resilience. Joy reinforces the value of incremental progress. When we recognize emotions as *signals* instead of *distractions*, we gain the ability to lead ourselves with intention rather than reaction.

Emotion may start as a feeling, but when cultivated consciously, it becomes a strategy. (You might want to read that one again.)

Emotion keeps you working when the payoff isn't visible yet. Emotion gives weight to your goals, clarity to your priorities, and persistence to your vision.

In short, emotion turns effort into endurance.

That's the kind of emotional fuel we need to power us through the transformation from comfort seekers to Reality Benders.

CULTIVATE YOUR INTERNAL CATALYST

So how do you tap into that emotional fuel and create your internal catalyst?

Mine the past.

Similar to using your imagination, you most likely already mine your past without realizing it. Every time you remember an experience, create an opinion about it, and use that opinion to determine how you want to act, that's mining the past. In practice, it tends to work one of two ways: You recall a time when you did something that resulted in a positive outcome, so you act in the same or a similar way to bring about another positive outcome. Or you relive a terrible moment and promise to do differently next time.

I started planning my wife's birthday months in advance. While it was a lot of work, it made her so happy to see everyone who could come, and she loved going out to her favorite restaurant. I should go ahead and set a reminder for next year.

Or:

I brought my work frustration home from the office. I yelled at my son when he asked if he could take the trash out later instead of now, and it really upset him. Taking out the trash wasn't an emergency. It could've waited. I was just still so angry from the meeting. I should find a way to let my bad attitude go before I walk in the door. And I should apologize to my son…

This is the kind of mining the past we do all the time. We reflect, interpret, and decide how to act in the next similar situation. When it comes to bending your reality, think of it like this: R.I.D. (reflect, interpret, decide) yourself of your old reality so that you can step into your new reality.

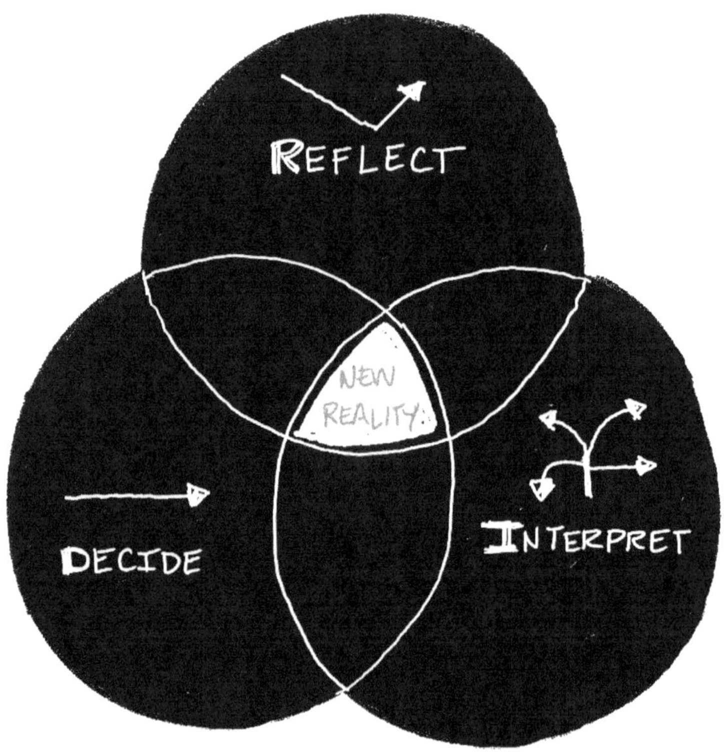

That's too easy, Greg. It can't be that easy. Just think about my past and choose to act differently, and then I can create a whole new reality? I'm not buying it…

Yes and no.

I teach a class on self-awareness, and I always start by asking everyone to raise their hand if they think self-awareness is hard. Everybody almost always raises their hand. Then I say, "Raise your hand if you think you ever reach 100 percent self-awareness."

In every moment of growth, there's tension between where you are and where you're going. Emotion bridges that gap. It carries your future self through the discomfort of transition until your mindset catches up.

Nobody raises their hand. Why is that? Because it requires so much of us.

If you want to bend your reality, you must identify the *thinking* that is creating the reality you currently have. But that's just the first step of the process. Then you have to determine the thinking that *needs to change* in order to bring about your new vision. Next, you have to pinpoint the counterproductive and often subconscious actions that are roadblocks to your new reality.

But you're not done yet.

Next comes analysis: What new actions should you take to create that new reality? How should you behave differently? This is what separates those who only dream of transformation from those who live it. Emotional intelligence—the ability to understand and harness your emotions—becomes the ultimate internal catalyst. When you reflect on past experiences, you're really decoding the emotional patterns that shaped your beliefs and behaviors. Recognizing these patterns enables you not just to change what you think but to rewire what you feel in response to challenges.

In every moment of growth, there's tension between where you are and where you're going. Emotion bridges that gap. It carries your future self through the discomfort of transition until your mindset catches up. Once you see emotion as an ally rather than the enemy, you stop fighting your feelings and start translating them into forward motion.

So now the final step: Determine what emotions are needed to fuel you to keep going, to keep acting without evidence of manifestation when you hit the roadblocks, when the frustration arises, when the result you want doesn't happen when you want it.

You need the fuel to keep the faith that change will come. Your emotions are that fuel.

But, there's another component at work here too: imagination.

Emotion provides the energy; imagination provides the direction.

Imagination allows us to *see, feel, and even experience* what doesn't yet exist.

A concrete example of this might be the positive feeling you feel after all that hard work in the gym when you know that you lifted a heavier weight and you *feel strong* on the inside. The numbers on the scale don't matter. You know you went to the gym when you didn't feel like it. You struggled to start. You ignored the looks. And now, you've lifted something heavy that is your new personal best. That's the kind of feeling you have to tap into as you start to bend your reality. That scream-from-the-top-of-your-lungs, "Holy-crap-I-can't-believe-I-just-did-that!" kind of emotion is what bends your reality and changes your life.

Emotion provides the energy; imagination provides the direction. Emotion is the fuel that sustains effort through uncertainty, but imagination is the compass that keeps us moving toward something greater. The two form a partnership: one powers the engine, the other steers the wheel. Without imagination, emotion burns out in frustration. Without emotion, imagination remains a daydream. Together, they create momentum that bends reality.

Imagination is not fantasy; it is the architecture for possibilities. Without imagination, we never could have walked on the moon. Every breakthrough, business, invention, and movement began as a mental picture created by someone who dared to imagine, who dared to ask, "What if?"

To construct a new reality cycle, you have to imagine a reality different from the one you have today. You have to create the vision of what life could be—your experience and knowledge must not limit that—and then ask the right questions. You have to create that architecture of possibilities.

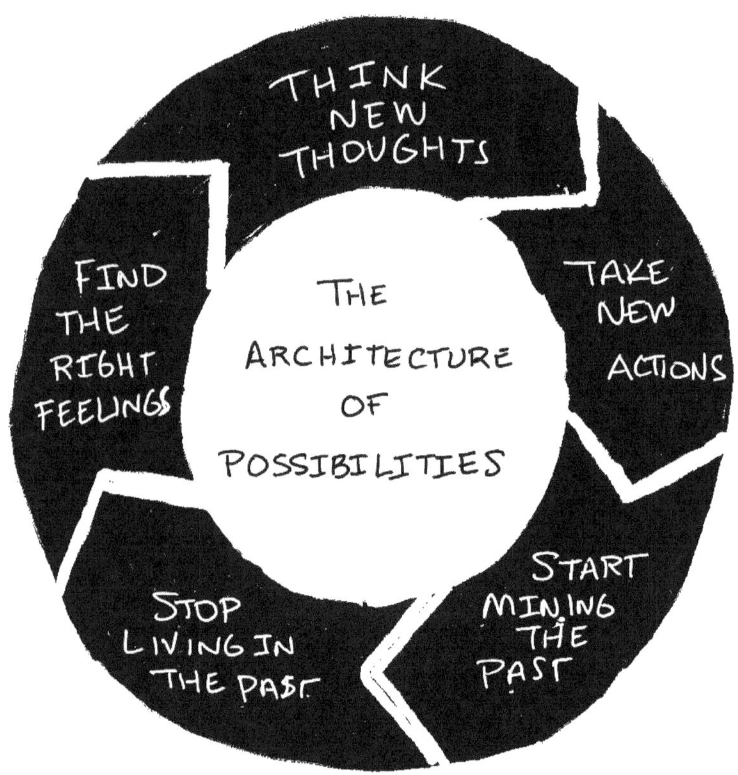

- **Think new thoughts.** How do I need to think differently to bring that reality to life?

- **Take new actions.** What do I need to do differently than I'm doing now?

- **Start mining the past.** What do I already know from past experience that can help me believe this new reality is possible?

- **Stop living in the past.** What do I already know from my past experience that is getting in the way of my new reality?

- **Feel the right feelings.** What emotion will I feel when I arrive there—and what emotion can I remember from my past that connects me to that feeling now?

These questions invite us to align our imagination with our emotional memory. That's where transformation begins. This is part of the process of mining the past, not living in it.

When we mine the past, we discover the emotional resources that have already carried us through adversity—the proof that we can endure, innovate, and overcome. Imagination then projects that strength forward, forming a vivid picture of what's next. While some of us have strong, positive memories that keep us going, like Dolly Parton, negative memories can motivate us, too, when we revisit them with purpose rather than pain. The memory of heartbreak may teach us how much reconciliation is worth. The sting of a failed business can ignite determination to lead more wisely the next time. As Tony Robbins put it, people will often do more to avoid pain than to gain pleasure.

So why not consciously use both pain and pleasure to drive progress?

Emotion gives us the *why*; imagination gives us the *what*. Emotion supplies the energy; imagination organizes that energy into vision. Every person who's ever reshaped their life began with these two in alignment. When imagination and emotion work in synergy, thinking begins to shift. And as new thoughts repeat, they embed new beliefs. Those beliefs, in turn, drive new behaviors—which generate new experiences. That cycle of thought, belief, behavior, and experience solidifies into a *new reality cycle*.

Consider this: Thinking alone can start change, but it cannot sustain it. Belief sustains change, and belief forms when the mind's imagination and the heart's emotion start speaking the same language. You begin to believe something not just because you think it's possible, but because you can feel it as true.

This is why people who succeed against all odds rarely lack imagination—they *see* what others can't. They allow themselves to experience, emotionally and mentally, the life they're building long before it arrives. Imagination activates curiosity; emotion gives it stamina. When frustration hits, imagination reminds us where we're going. When doubt creeps in, emotion remembers how it feels to win.

As you reimagine your own reality cycle:

- Use imagination to form the blueprint of the life you desire—your finish line, in vivid color.

- Use emotion to fuel your resolve—the inner fire that stays lit when results are delayed.

Most people live in outdated cycles not because they lack goals, but because they've stopped envisioning. They settle for what they can measure instead of what they can imagine. But reality bending requires imagination without limits.

Free your imagination from the burden of proof or permission. Picture the life you're meant to live—relationships healed, purpose fulfilled, contribution fully realized. Imagination doesn't ignore obstacles or problems; it gives meaning to the effort required to overcome them. Every time you hold that image in your mind and connect it emotionally to your reason for being, you reinforce the neural pathways that make belief possible. And belief, once embedded, reshapes reality.

Every great transformation starts this way—first through thought, then in feeling, and finally in the physical world around you.

A powerful practice to get started mining your past with purpose is to revisit defining moments—your greatest trials and triumphs—and reinterpret them through the lens of appreciation. Don't relive it, mine it. Ask yourself: *What lessons did each experience teach? What emotional strength did I develop because of it?* With that awareness, look at even your most painful chapter and say, *That wasn't a setback; it was a setup.* What once broke you can now fuel you.

Remember: Imagination reassigns meaning; emotion fuels movement. Together, they create the internal conditions necessary to shift your beliefs and construct your new reality cycle. Every great transformation starts this way—first through thought, then in feeling, and finally in the physical world around you.

If you find yourself losing hope or momentum, revisit your vision and re-engage your emotion. *Imagine* the person you are becoming. *Feel* the gratitude as if it's your current reality. This is how visionaries, innovators, and leaders create futures that others call impossible.

You *are* a visionary—but only if you'll allow yourself to be one.

*Adversity reveals
the edge of your
current identity.*

*Growth begins when
you refuse to stay there.*

*Setbacks are not
endings—they are
bending points.*

chapter six

THINK, DIFFERENT

rom a young age, Eddie Murphy moved in the direction of his dream to be a performer and get on television, even at a time when there were almost no black actors on the small screen.[6] He was always a funny kid with a vision of making people laugh. In the documentary, *Being Eddie*, he recalls that around age thirteen, he started saying he was going to be famous by the time he was eighteen. It was his mantra. "And I really, really, really, really believed it with every fiber," he says.[7]

When he was seventeen, he became a comic; when he was eighteen, he was doing standup in comedy clubs, and when he was nineteen, he was cast on *Saturday Night Live*.

His mother admitted that as a kid, she tried to discourage him from pursuing a career in comedy and entertainment, but he did it anyway. He couldn't hold himself back. In less than ten years, he'd created the reality he'd dreamed of living.

At that point, Eddie could've said, "I'm funny. I'm a comic. This is what I'll do for the rest of my life because this is who I am," even though he was only nineteen years old. Sounds absurd, right? Especially as we've had the benefit of seeing all the different things he's done and all the different identities he's adopted along the way.

However, as this example shows, once you've created your desired reality, you've also created a certain mindset and subsequently, an identity that supports this it. (Ponder that one for a minute.) So ask yourself this question: *How many people do I know right now, including me, who say they can't do something different or new because they've been the same way and have done the same thing for so long?*

It usually sounds like this: "I've worked at ABC Corporation for twenty, twenty-five years. It's stable. I have a retirement account and health insurance. Why do something new? This is who I am," or "I've worked in HR for thirty years. I don't know anything about starting a business. That's not who I am."

What story are you telling yourself right now about who you think you are?

Instead of becoming stuck in his identity as a stage comic and television performer, Eddie Murphy changed. He adapted and adopted a new mindset and a new identity: movie star.

How could he take that leap?

Partly because film producer Jeffrey Katzenberg presented it to him as an opportunity to do something *in addition to*, not *instead of* what he had been doing.[8] Eddie the Movie Star wouldn't replace Eddie the Stand-Up Comedian, but rather, he would add a new layer to his identity. So Murphy took a chance and has continued adding layers, adopting new mindsets and identities, and bending his reality every step of the way—and so can you.

You're on the edge of something incredible, but there is a point in every transformation—right after the vision is set, the emotions are awakened, and the imagination starts expanding—when progress slows and momentum dies. Not because the goal is wrong. Not because you lack motivation. But because you've maxed out the identity that has carried you this far. This is where most Reality Cycles lose momentum and eventually fail.

People whose Reality Cycles look like this need to understand something: They can change their habits, their routines, their goals and ambitions, but if they never change the person performing those actions, reality won't change. Thoughts, emotions, beliefs, and actions cannot grow beyond the identity holding them. Identity is the quiet operating system that runs your reality cycle, thereby running your life. It filters every thought you entertain, every emotion you trust, every belief you defend, every action that feels "like you."

Most people never fully realize one fundamental truth: We do not construct identities from potential; we construct them from familiarity. We are not wired for expansion and growth; we are wired for survival through comfort, stability, and predictability.

Your brain's primary job is not expansion; it is safety. And safety lives in familiarity.

Reality Benders have to buck this trend in order to create a new identity.

Your identity, unless deliberately rewritten, will always drift toward the version of you that requires the least emotional risk. And that is typically the familiar self, the predictable self, the "I already know how to be this person" self. That self may not be your highest and best self, but it is the easiest.

But hear me say this—the easiest self is the sworn enemy of the imagined self.

The familiar identity *always* feels safer than the future identity.

Throughout this book, we've talked about the existence of infinite possibilities and versions of you. There was once a version of you who (at least to some degree) wanted the life you're living today. That person had your same name, looked at least somewhat like the person you see in the mirror every morning, but had a different mindset and a different identity. They aspired to be *the you* in the now. The man who navigated the 2008 financial crisis shares the same DNA as the man writing these words today. Seventeen years later we are very different people, and yet, the 2008 Greg made the 2025 Greg possible because what happened then propelled me to become a new version of myself and create a new reality now.

Right here, right now, you must cultivate a new mindset and identity to bend your reality. It's a continuous journey of self-discovery because every time you want to create a new reality, you must become a new you. Period. You establish a new mindset and a new identity. You must think new thoughts and take new actions to create new outcomes that feed back into the Reality Cycle. These new thoughts, new actions, and new beliefs eventually become new beliefs, new behaviors, and new experiences.

Even as I write this book, I've gone on a new journey to create a new reality. Trust me when I say that this content is *so different* from what I've written before that I've continually had to push back against the old identity that wants to keep me comfortable and safe. I've had to question and challenge my thoughts, I've had to rewire my neurons, and it's working. I'm creating my next reality *with you*. Isn't that an amazing thought? I may never meet you, but together, we're creating a new reality that benefits us both.

You've got the fuel—emotions and imagination. You've got the map—the Reality Cycle. You've even felt the emotional surge that says, "This is real. This is mine."

So now I'll ask you: *Who do you think you are … to live this life?*

Be honest, when you picture that future version of you—on stage, in the C-suite, debt-free, fit, working remotely, leading a dynamic team, unstoppable—does a little voice whisper, "Yeah, but that's not me? That's for people smarter and more talented than me."

I know I've thought those words and felt that way before.

That voice you're hearing? That's your *current* identity talking, trying to weasel its way into your thoughts and wreck your new reality cycle. It doesn't care about your vision. It doesn't care about your feelings. It only cares about familiarity. It cares about pulling you back into a cycle that no longer serves you and your new vision.

What happens when your imagination outruns your identity? When your reality starts growing, but your current self stays stuck in the past? That gap is what I call Identity Lag, and it's where 99 percent of Reality Cycles collapse.

To achieve an "identity upgrade," you have to ask:

> *Who must I become to sustain this new reality?*
> *What beliefs are creating the identity that holds me hostage?*

What old version of me needs to be released—today?
And how do I act my way into a self I don't yet believe in?

You're not just bending reality now. You're becoming the person it requires.

The destination isn't a place—it's a person; it's the next you.

IDENTITY LAG

The conflict lies between who you're becoming and who you still believe you are. In Chapter 4, I shared the moment on the plane when I saw someone reading my book. By that point in my career, I was an author. I had the books and sales to prove it, but my identity still lagged in the old, familiar version of me: the businessman who occasionally wrote things. Even though my reality had grown, my identity lagged behind. Identity Lag happens when:

- Your reality grows faster than your identity;
- Your imagination expands faster than your beliefs; or
- Your potential outpaces your comfort zone.

Identity Lag is also where the reality cycle can actually shrink because it's impossible to sustain a new reality with an identity grounded in the old one. This is the moment when most people retreat. It's not out of fear or from incapacity, but rather it's from the intense gravitational pull of familiarity and safety. Identity Lag is like a black hole that sucks you in if you get too close. It's the reason imagination and the right emotional anchor are so important: Not only will they pull you through when you want to quit, but they will also help you break free from your old identity.

The human brain has three primary functions: conserve energy, avoid risk, and to return to familiarity and safety. Growth violates all three.

Trying something new? Risky.

Changing a belief? Risky.

Creating a new identity? Existential threat.

And all of it takes a lot of energy.

So the brain doesn't shield you from failure—it shields you from change. We've already mentioned that self-sabotage isn't fear of success; it's your brain pulling you back to the familiar self, the one it already knows how to operate.

Seeking comfort is natural. It is safe.

Becoming a Reality Bender is not natural. It is intentional.

And to get there, you must *think the new thoughts* that build your new mindset.

INFINITE POSSIBLE REALITIES AND INFINITE POSSIBLE IDENTITIES

What do a figure skater, a magazine editor, and a fashion designer have in common? They're all Vera Wang.

When you hear her name, you may be quick to associate Vera Wang with women's clothing, but she encapsulates the art of building a new mindset and new identity to create a new reality. At a 2005 *Women's Wear Daily* summit, she said, "For nearly four decades, my life has been defined—some would say consumed—by fashion, but my career has been every bit as much about adversity as it has about passion, coupled with the necessary willingness to accept change."[9]

As a child, she dreamed of becoming an Olympic figure skater, but after failing twice to make the team in the late 1960s, she took a job at *Vogue* magazine. She continued to work there for almost twenty years, rising in the ranks from editor to director and more, with her sights set on becoming the next editor in chief. Unfortunately, she was passed over for the position. So in her late thirties, she pivoted once again and went to work as a designer for Ralph Lauren. But it wasn't until she turned forty and opened her first bridal boutique in the Carlyle Hotel in New York City that she became *the* Vera Wang we know today.

In the world of fashion, Wang has done everything from designing celebrity and A-lister wedding gowns to red carpet fashions, Olympian figure skating outfits to everyday women's wear with her Simply Vera Vera Wang line. She's done runway shows, designed accessories, won the Council of Fashion Designers of America's Lifetime Achievement Award, and has even partnered with Chopin Vodka on a line of spirits. And every time she's pivoted, she's had to create a new reality. She's had to think differently about who *she* thinks she is and about what *she* believes she can do.

What's more wild than a life that spans so many different realities? The fact that this level of reality bending isn't unique to her. Like having strong emotional anchors that drive them, most successful people have reinvented their identities and reimagined their lives in big, big ways. They couldn't have done the amazing things they've done if they hadn't pushed through the pain of thinking differently about themselves.

Can you imagine Amazon if Jeff Bezos had only stuck with selling books? Or what about the world of food or entertainment without Julia Child or Martha Stewart? The artist Grandma Moses didn't even start painting until she was almost eighty years old![10] Before that she cleaned houses and worked on farms.

You can change your mind about who you think you are and what you think you can do at any point.

You can change your mind about who you think you are and what you think you can do at any point. (You might want to read that one again and underline it.) You have the vision for your next reality cycle. You have the emotional fuel. All that's left is imagining the next version of you, the you who's already living that next reality cycle. To create your new identity and mindset, you just need to start with a new thought.

SHAKE UP YOUR NEURONS TO WRITE A NEW STORY

Have you ever thought about what a thought is? We've touched on how powerful they are and how they work in the Reality Cycle process, but what are they really? Do they actually exist? Do they take up space? Indulge me a bit because this is pretty cool.

Scientists and researchers are still figuring it out, and they don't agree on any one theory at this point, yet, when we boil all of these ideas down, a thought is not a physical thing: It's some form of energy—electrical pulses, electromagnetic waves, photons, electrochemical reactions, quantum, or something else.[11, 12, 13] As these energy pulses travel the pathways connecting and activating the different parts of our brain, they form relationships with each other.

Donald Hebb, a Canadian psychologist, studied these neural activities and developed **Hebb's Law**, which says: **"Neurons that fire together wire together."**[14] So if you repeatedly activate the same nerve cells, each time they turn on, it will be easier for them to work in unison. Eventually, those neurons form a long-term relationship and become hardwired. That's how we form habits, for better or worse.

In relation to the Reality Cycle, when you think a specific thought and do a specific action time and again, the bond strengthens between the neurons related to the thought (belief) and those of the action (behavior). In this way, the next time you think the thought, you automatically perform the action, or vice versa.

Once you've developed this learned connection, it becomes encoded in your brain, where it's transferred into your brain's long-term storage. At this point, it becomes an embedded belief and the basis for your identity.[15] Once it's a belief system, it also becomes a solid lens (how you see and interpret the world), and the corresponding Reality Cycle will manifest.

As you can see in the Reality Cycle diagram, that's how you move from the short-term, conscious, surface cycle (thoughts > actions > outcomes) to the long-term, subconscious, internal cycle (belief systems> embedded behaviors > life experiences). This also ties back to Chapter 2 and the Commitment and Consistency Principle. You will unconsciously continue to think and act in ways that reinforce your embedded belief system.

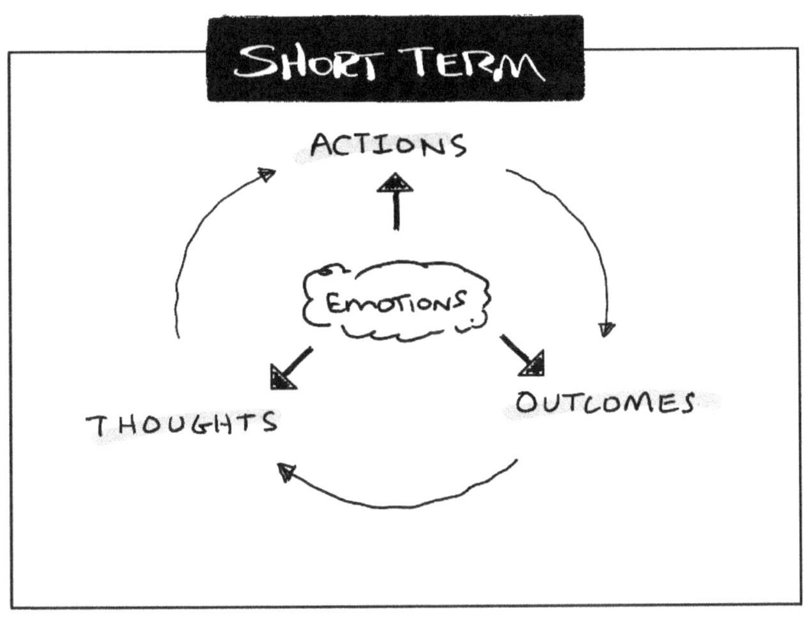
SHORT TERM
ACTIONS
EMOTIONS
THOUGHTS
OUTCOMES

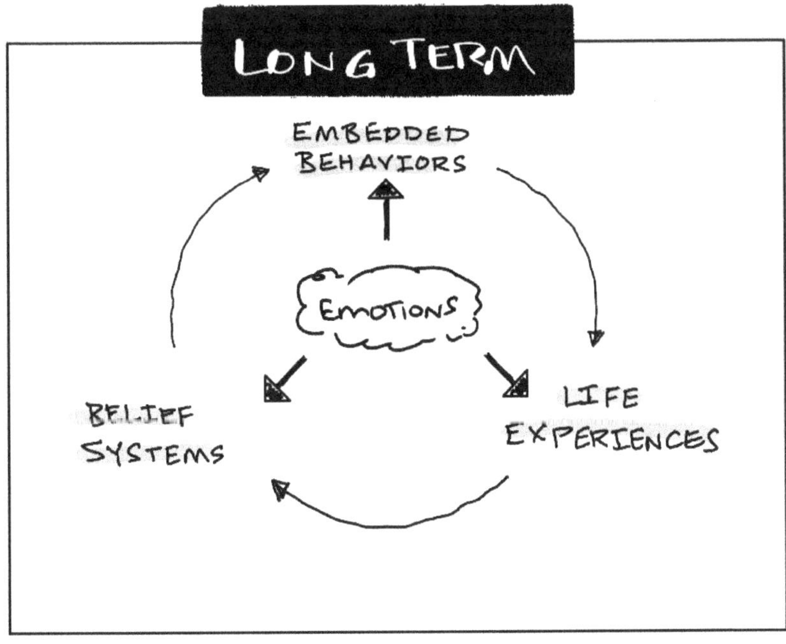
LONG TERM
EMBEDDED BEHAVIORS
EMOTIONS
BELIEF SYSTEMS
LIFE EXPERIENCES

It takes a lot of mental discipline to influence our thoughts because they happen all the time. When they're part of our embedded belief system, we feel like we can't control how they cause us to feel or act. While we do generate some thoughts ourselves, most of the time, thinking is an unconscious process. Most of the time, the brain creates a thought in response to a stimulus—one that we may or may not realize we've encountered.[16] That makes thoughts *immensely* powerful.

This means that, in order to change your Reality Cycle, you must *disrupt* the system creating your current reality, identity, and mindset, and recognize the pattern of thinking and actions holding you back from the next version of you. This is where it can get tricky: You must *consciously choose a different thought to build your new identity and take a different action.*

But you're not doing this alone—you have your imagination and emotional anchor to fuel your transformation.

Before we move on, I'm going to ask you to do something because I know this is a difficult aspect of becoming a Reality Bender. But after you've been bending a while, this process of thinking a new thought will become part of your embedded belief system, and it will become easier to believe in something new over and over again.

Remember the story about my roommate and the picture of the Porsche taped to his mirror, his face covering that of the model in the car? I'm going to ask you to find your Porsche picture and tape it to your mirror. Find an image of whatever makes you think of your new reality cycle and the person who lives that reality, and put it in a place where you'll look at it multiple times a day. Maybe that means you make copies and place them on your desk, on the bathroom mirror, on the refrigerator, wherever. I want you to look at it and think about it whenever you're feeling stuck or whenever you want to quit. If you start thinking, "I can't do this..." go look at those pictures.

This simple action does two powerful things. First, it disrupts the neural circuitry that would hold you back and helps you begin to recognize the moment you fall back into that old, outdated habit. It refocuses you on the you you are becoming and gives you the pause you need to choose your new thought. Second, it activates your imagination and triggers your emotional anchor, reminding you why you're doing this in the first place.

Look at the picture and feel the feelings of the next you.

Imagine what your days are like and how life will be different.

Let that settle into your mind, then come back to finish reading this chapter.

CULTIVATE THE MINDSET TO POWER YOUR TRANSFORMATION

The crowd roared as Michael Phelps, his teammates, and competitors walked across the humid pool deck in Beijing in 2008. His head down, earbuds in, and pumping music to help him focus, Phelps played through the next few minutes in his mind. He'd line up behind his lane number with the other swimmers, remove his warm-up jacket and earbuds, pull down his goggles, then step up to the blocks, flap his long arms to stretch out, and take a deep breath before the buzzer sounded. He'd done this hundreds—shoot, *thousands*—of times before.

The buzzer would announce the start of the race, and he would launch himself into the warm water below—fingertips, head, shoulders, torso, legs, feet—kick! He knew the exact number of breaths he needed to take, how his arms would feel as they moved in and out of the water, how his feet would press against the ceramic wall of the pool as he turned. It was only him and the clock. Nothing else mattered.

As he visualized the race, he'd also think about everything that could go wrong. What if he missed a breath? What if his feet slipped on the turn? What if he didn't push off hard enough on the initial leap into the pool? And he'd go through his list of solutions. By the time he stepped up for the actual race, he could feel the weight of the gold medal in his palm, feel the smooth edge of it as he kissed it, the American national anthem playing as the Stars and Stripes rose above the podium. He could succeed. He *would* succeed.

Choose your mindset carefully. You cannot live in a future you do not believe you are allowed to inhabit.

He was a winner, and that's just what winners do.

What separates those with potential to succeed from those, like Michael Phelps, who do succeed? What separates would-be Benders from Bending Masters? One word: Mindset. It's all about thinking the right thoughts, which create the right identity for the moment.

Mindset is everything. It is the embedded belief system that drives your reality, and it creates the foundation of your identity. If you think you can, you will, and whoever you think you are, you will become (or continue to be.) And the energy of those thoughts will create the corresponding reality.

Choose your mindset carefully. You cannot live in a future you do not believe you are allowed to inhabit. In other words, a mindset built on comfort will work hard to minimize risk and maximize safety. It's a mindset that will keep you stuck in *this* reality. It will always try to sabotage a Reality Cycle built on imagination. It will tell you:

- "People like me don't speak up."
- "I'm not creative."
- "I'm not very good with money."
- "I don't do well with pressure."
- "My parents wouldn't approve."
- "I can't afford it."
- "It's just genetics."
- "What if I fail?"

To break free of the wrong mindset (which, by the way, sounds a lot like excuses) and cultivate the mindset that will support your desired cycle, you need to activate your imagination and inhabit the vision of that future. Every time you do this, you weaken the old neural pathways and strengthen the new ones. Every time you do this, you move one step closer to that next reality and one step farther away from the old one. Every time you do this, you take the next action that will manifest your new cycle because you will believe that's just who you are. If that's who you are, then that's just what you do. You become a self-perpetuating Reality Bender.

These are the most important truths of the Reality Cycle: **Mindset is the foundation for identity, and identity dictates what you will allow yourself to think, what you will allow yourself to feel, and what you will allow yourself to imagine.**

OUTDATED REALITY: FAMILIAR SELF	NEXT REALITY: FUTURE SELF
REJECTS BOLD THOUGHTS	WELCOMES THEM
SUPPRESSES BIG EMOTIONS	AMPLIFIES THEM
SHRINKS IMAGINATION	EXPANDS IMAGINATION
DEFENDS LIMITING BELIEFS	REWRITES LIMITING BELIEFS
PERMITS ONLY SAFE ACTIONS	DEMANDS DARING ACTIONS

When mindset shifts, everything else follows.

So how do you shift your mindset? Change your thoughts.

THE THOUGHT BENDING MATRIX

Every cycle begins with a story—a story about who you think you are and how you think the world works. That story isn't true because it's accurate; it's true because it's familiar. People stay in the same jobs, in the same patterns, in the same frustrations, not because they love them but because they know them.

Your mind whispers the same predictable narrative; your thoughts repeat it; your emotions agree with it; your beliefs reinforce it; and your actions follow it. The old mindset always wins unless you recreate it. This is why thought management alone doesn't work. We've got to eradicate the old thoughts from the root and implant the new thoughts that support your new identity.

That's where The Thought Bending Matrix comes in:

THE THOUGHT-BENDING MATRIX

	DIRECTION			
AWARENESS	BACKWARD	FORWARD (MISALIGNED)	FORWARD (LIMITED)	ALIGNED, EMPOWERED
EXAMINED THOUGHTS	AVOIDANCE • You play small on purpose • You have strong protective beliefs • You self-censor "I don't think it's possible..."	CONSCIOUS MISFIRE • Good intentions wrong target • Goals don't align w/ desired reality "If I just hustle harder..."	KNOWN CEILING • Imposter feelings • Desire vs deserve mismatch "I know I'm holding back..."	REALITY-BENDING THOUGHTS • Empowering thoughts • Aligned belief systems • Momentum w/ purpose "I can't be stopped!"
UNEXAMINED THOUGHTS	REFLEXIVE THOUGHTS • Shame scripts run by default • Crippling self doubt "I can't..."	UNCONSCIOUS DRIFT • Busy, but unfocused • People-pleasing • Old patterns "I'll do what I've always done..."	HIDDEN CEILING • Fearing success • Past experiences cap future • Quiet self-limiting beliefs "I'll do just enough..."	ACCIDENTAL MOMENTUM • Optimism without intention • Natural talent carries you "It seems to work. I'll stay the course..."
INTENTIONALITY	DRIFTING THOUGHTS			DIRECTED THOUGHTS

REALITY — BENT / BASIC

Many people, if not most, spend a lot of time on the bottom of the matrix with automatic, unchallenged thoughts. These thoughts are reactive and often negative. They work to keep you right where you are. They don't like change and they don't like risk. They are familiar and comforting.

Within this level, your thoughts may be reflexive and so move you backwards. They may keep you complacent, and so you build someone else's dream reality instead of your own—you're moving forward, but the reality is misaligned with what you want (if you know what you want).

However, through a force of unsustainable will, you *might* make a few moves to the right to create a different reality, but at some point, you'll stop as your thoughts create an unconscious, hidden ceiling, so you'll stall out. And then there's the happy accident—as you drift through life, you might create a pretty good reality. It's not the one you imagined, or maybe even want per se, but it's not terrible, so you'll take it. You move forward without intention.

As people become aware of what they're thinking, even if they don't yet know why, they move into the top of the matrix. They may avoid risks on purpose, creating a safe, comfortable reality that moves them away from their full potential. They might have a specific reality in mind, but take the wrong actions, and so they're sort of moving laterally, drifting away from their desired reality.

At some point, they may adjust their actions in line with their thinking and start creating the reality they always imagined—until imposter syndrome sets in, and then they'll hold themselves back from going the full distance because who are they to get everything they want?

But the sweet spot, the place where the Benders live, is when they align their belief system (mindset) with their thoughts (identity) to take empowered actions. That's where you want to be!

I realize that seems like it's a lot of ground to cover, but it is absolutely possible to start out in the bottom, backward corner of the matrix and move into the upper, "Master Bender" quadrant. I've certainly lived it, and I've seen and helped others do it. That's why I'm writing this book. It just requires a certain amount of mindfulness.

If you're groaning right now, I get it. When people talk about mindfulness, they usually follow it up with, "I meditate for sixty minutes a day, have a morning journaling practice, and drink green smoothies." That's great. Practitioners and researchers alike know that meditation is a powerful tool. It can reduce your stress and anxiety, improve your sleep, and increase your focus. It also physically improves your brain functioning. But like everything, it's not for everyone. So I'm not going to ask you to figure out how to meditate for sixty minutes a day or even at all, if it's not for you. (If you want to, please go for it.) But I always err on the side of highly practical, quickly actionable work. So we're going to cultivate momentary mindfulness throughout the day, every time a thought related to your future pops into your head.

Most of us will end up bending reality while still living in our current reality. It'll feel like you're standing with one foot in each reality because we often can't stop everything we're doing and just jump into the next one. We have to build it piece by piece. This means there will be certain times of day you're thinking about it and working on it. That's when I want you to practice this momentary mindfulness.

For example, if your next reality is about building your own business, you'll have several steps before it's ready. Maybe you need to find a lawyer to do the paperwork, create a website and marketing materials, etc. When you run into obstacles or you're too tired to work on the business or you don't know what to do next, those thoughts will start popping into your head. When they do, remember R.C.A.:

Recognize the thought. Does it move you forward or backward? Where does it live on the chart?

Challenge it. Is it true? If so, where's the proof? Ask yourself, "Why am I thinking this?" And keep asking why until you get to the belief behind the thought.

Adjust your thinking. If this thought lives in the Reactive, Unconscious Drift quadrant, what needs to change to move forward and up? How would the New You respond? How would the New You living your new reality reframe the situation?

Remember, these outdated thoughts are aligned with the old you, your old reality. They are loyal to that misaligned mindset and identity to a fault, and they will say anything they have to in order to stop you from changing and growing. This is your moment of Identity Lag. Every time that happens, R.C.A. the thought, spend a few minutes living in your vision for the future, and allow the excitement and emotion to push forward.

Do this until it becomes a habit, and congratulations: You've just stepped into your future self. You named the identity. You got rid of the old one. You've defeated Identity Lag. You even took that one courageous action that your familiar self never would have touched.

But here's the real deal: Mindset without action is just a costume. You can say, "I'm a disciplined creator" all day, but if your habits don't match, then you're still living in yesterday's reality.

So what's the next step? How do you make your new mindset stick? How do you turn a one-time courageous move into your default operating system? And what's the difference between trying to change and designing your inner self so change is inevitable?

Replace the architecture. Benders don't simply modify behavior—they build the systems that make the new reality inevitable and automatic.

This is the time to turn beliefs into actions that become embedded behaviors.

You're not hoping to change now. You're actively engineering it.

Belief shows up as behavior. Every choice is a vote for the identity you are building.

chapter seven

NEW ACTION, NEW CYCLE

o this day, the Empire State Building remains a prime example of project management brilliance. A couple of months before Wall Street crashed in 1929, a handful of building firms in New York City created proposals to construct the world's tallest skyscraper in a competition dubbed "the Race for the Sky." The enthusiasm was contagious, and half a dozen businessmen and former politicians created Empire State Inc. to enter the fray.

There were many reasons these men wanted to build the world's tallest skyscraper:

- ambition
- revitalization of the declining Waldorf-Astoria hotel area of Manhattan
- to create more office and living space
- And because many of them had ties to General Motors, they *really* wanted to beat Walter Chrysler of the Chrysler Corporation.

The world had just survived World War I, the Spanish flu pandemic, and the waning years of Prohibition. Everyone was ready to celebrate life, and constructing massive buildings was a way to create visual monuments and striking symbols of everything they'd survived.

And then, just when things were getting interesting, Wall Street crashed.

Of the firms that initially submitted building proposals, only two continued on: those behind the Chrysler Building and the Empire State Building. Both groups were well-funded and could afford to hire the finest construction crews in the city, which suddenly had open calendars thanks to the crash.

The Empire State Building—the "Eighth Wonder of the World"—was conceived and completed in a whirlwind eighteen months, a feat that has rarely, if ever, happened since. To give you some perspective, the original 1 World Trade Center, or the North Tower, stood at 1,368 feet and officially took the title of "world's tallest building" from the Empire State Building in 1970, but its construction took about six years. So how could a structure built more than thirty years earlier (and that's almost as tall) have been created so much faster?

The right planning and execution—and a little bit of healthy pressure.

As the old Waldorf-Astoria Hotel was torn down and the site prepped for building the Empire State Building, the architects at Shreve, Lamb, and Harmon, headed by William F. Lamb, got to work designing. The problem came with upping the ante: Whenever someone got wind of what they were doing with the Chrysler Building, Empire State Inc. had to add a few floors or raise the roof—anything to guarantee that they would have the tallest building.

However, you can't keep changing plans forever, or nothing will get built.

Ultimately, the team realized it was going to be plan #16 or bust.

The original agreements for the Empire State Building stipulated that it had to be built and opened within eighteen months. This meant the architects and suppliers, construction crews, and contractors had to play nice and work pretty much concurrently during many phases of the process. To use the terminology we've developed in this book, they worked the future-back approach. The agreement forced a mindset that this *could* be done in eighteen months, so it would be. With the future vision locked in place, this then ignited the imagination of how to make that timeline possible.

Architects and committees finalized the design plans. Within days of the steel suppliers winning contracts, the excavation for the new site began, even though crews were still demolishing the old Waldorf-Astoria hotel occupying the lot. As soon as the site was cleared, workers began to lay out the foundations. Ironworkers placed the first steel columns in the few completed footings as others completed the rest of the footings. Prefabricating and shipping much of the steel structures for the building made the work go faster.

As the building grew taller and construction moved higher and higher into the sky, cafes opened on various floors so workers didn't have to venture far for food and drink. Crews kept additional building supplies in the basement, and on the first few floors to keep the work going. In fact, because of the efficiency of the process, at one point workers were able to build fourteen floors in a ten-day period.

While the crews raced to finish every detail, the best thing happened: The Chrysler Building opened in 1930, *initially* winning the title of world's tallest skyscraper.

Why was this good for our heroes? Because it meant that the Chrysler Building was finished. No more changes or last-minute plans. Empire State Inc. suddenly had a clear height goal to beat: 1,046 feet. One final, last-minute plan revision added sixteen floors and other features to raise the height of the mast on the building.

With a roof height of 1,250 feet, the Empire State Building officially won the race and the coveted title when it opened to the public on May 1, 1931. And yes, eighteen months after the planners approved the initial designs, the Empire State Building opened its doors.

You may be wondering what this has to do with bending reality. I'll tell you.

Reality changes when belief-driven behavior becomes your new default.

The construction of a new Reality Cycle is very similar to the construction of the Empire State Building. You imagine a new future, rewrite limiting stories, activate a new identity, and even reconstruct your belief system. Yet reality won't shift *until behavior shifts*. Behavior becomes the steel frame supporting the cycle you're working so hard to create. Without it, there's nothing holding up your new cycle, and it will crumble away.

And we're not talking about a temporary shift in behavior.

Not "motivated" behavior.

Not behavior that depends on adrenaline, accountability, or pressure.

Reality changes when belief-driven behavior becomes your new default because belief-driven change lowers the internal resistance. Change then becomes easier. It becomes a source of renewal instead of distress.

Further, this new belief-driven behavior isn't created in a vacuum. Benders know that, most of the time, we don't just have a new thought once, and suddenly our beliefs and identity become what the new cycle needs. And we don't just do something new once and suddenly get the outcomes we want and create the new cycle overnight. This is a concurrent work-in-progress, like what the different crews and workers who built the Empire State Building experienced. This is finalizing the design while sourcing the steel and finishing the demolition on the pre-existing hotel so we have a place on which to build something new.

Until it becomes second nature, you will have to R.C.A. (recognize, challenge, and adjust) your thoughts *while* you act with intention to build the new cycle, over and over again. It won't be perfect every single time, but that's okay. That's part of the process as you shed your old cycle and step into the new.

Identity defines who you must become. Belief outlines what's possible. But behavior is where the intangible transforms into the inevitable.

Think about it like this: Identity defines who you must become. Belief outlines what's possible. But behavior is where the intangible transforms into the inevitable.

This is what Benders understand at a deeper level than everyone else: A new reality requires new embedded behaviors. New embedded behaviors require new beliefs. You're establishing and reinforcing the thoughts that become the embedded beliefs as the repeated actions become embedded behaviors.

In the last chapter, you started creating the new beliefs; now it's time to develop the new embedded behaviors that will build your new reality. Benders build the behavioral architecture that makes a new reality inevitable—not by a battle of wills, not through force, but through design.

THE REALITY CYCLE AND THE POWER OF ACTION

Imagine if the architects and engineers of the Empire State Building tried to build that massive structure using the pre-existing Waldorf-Astoria Hotel as the foundation. It would have saved time and money. It would've been a little difficult to line the West and East sections of the building up, as the Waldorf side of the hotel was 225 feet high while the Astoria side was 270 feet high with a 980-foot-long corridor connecting the two, but not impossible. At the very least, they would've needed to add about 1,000 feet of steel and stone to reach the ultimate height of the Empire State Building.

However, even if they could've set the modern behemoth on top of the old structures, the hotels had been built in 1893 and 1897. The building codes governing their construction were very different from those of the Empire State Building. And at a whopping 365,000 tons (or 730 million pounds), these old hotels would have provided a shaky foundation at best.

Constructing a new, modern building on top of an old, outdated foundation is like trying to change your life through willpower. You grind harder. You push through. You battle resistance. You cling to deteriorating motivation like your life depends on it. And yet, this is exactly how most people try to change their lives. But this sheer force will only work until the familiar identity and old belief structure reassert themselves—and believe me, they will reassert themselves. At some point, the "wagon" tips, habits revert, and then we label it a "failure." But it's never a failure; it's just building on a flawed foundation.

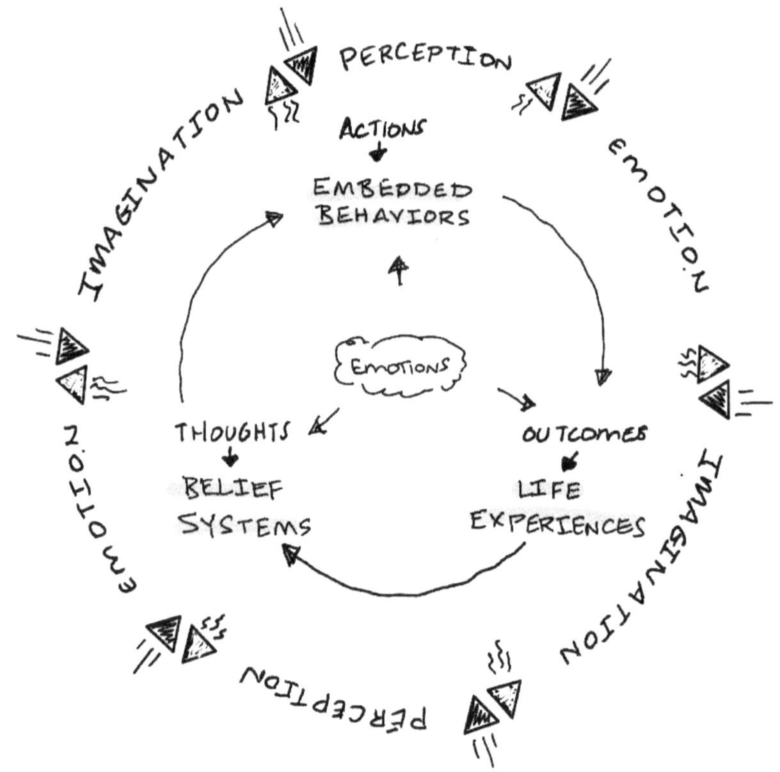

THE PERCEPTION EMOTION IMAGINATION EXCHANGE IS FUELED BY ACTION

THE OLD GOES IN

THE NEW GOES OUT

You can't sustain new behavior built on old beliefs. The structure eventually collapses.

Changing your life doesn't require more willpower … just a better loop.

Earlier in the book, you learned about the Reality Cycle flow, but now I want to deepen your understanding of how this works when you begin taking action toward your new reality.

Action is the **pivot point** on which everything turns. Action is where:

- Identity materializes
- Belief becomes embodied
- Imagination shifts from dream to movement
- Emotions convert to momentum
- Outcomes solidify into a new reality

Action is the first place where the internal world collides with the external world. **Action is not only the beginning of change, but it's also the physical expression of belief.** New beliefs create new actions, which create new cycles. Repeated actions (old or new) become the **embedded behaviors** that form your identity and shape what you believe is possible.

There is an exchange that happens. I call it the Perception Emotion Imagination Exchange. As you begin to take new actions, you bring your old perception, emotions, and imagination into the Reality Cycle. But as you take those actions, something amazing takes place. Your perception shifts, allowing you to see things differently (think back to Chapter 2 and bending a new lens for your new way of seeing). Your emotions grow, allowing you to feel your future more fully, and your imagination expands, allowing you to believe that new future is possible. But this exchange can't happen—won't happen—*until you act.*

You are constantly evolving into your most repeated behavior.

This is why Benders focus on building a behavioral *framework* rather than behavior *modification*. Building the right behavioral framework, establishing the right behavioral architecture, requires you to focus on the proper identity and then aligning beliefs and actions with that identity..

Behavior modification relies on force. Any resultant change will be temporary, exhausting, and fragile. *Behavioral architecture* thrives on alignment. Alignment is natural, automatic, and enduring. Reality Benders don't fight their old behaviors. They **replace the old belief structure** that gave those behaviors life with the new belief system that makes the new behaviors automatic and their new cycle inevitable.

Again, it's a deliberate exchange.

You must get rid of the old to make way for something new.

THE WISDOM OF BILL MURRAY

In the 1993 film *Groundhog Day*, weatherman Phil Connors, played by Bill Murray, finds himself trapped in a time loop. The plot is simple: For an unknown number of days, Phil wakes up over and over again on February 2 in Punxsutawney, Pennsylvania. Every morning, he hears Sonny and Cher sing "I Got You Babe" before trudging to the town center where he has to cover the Punxsutawney Phil Groundhog emergence—something he feels is beneath him, very beneath him.

All Phil wants to do is leave his small-town job behind for a bigger station and "more important" reporting. But every morning, he hears the stupid clock radio click on, Sonny and Cher serenading him with their pop love song.

At first he's distraught. How will life actually begin if he can never move forward? But then he realizes: There are no consequences for his actions! If he just starts over every day, he can do whatever he wants, from binge eating and drinking to thievery and more, and wake up on February 2 with nothing having changed.

As Phil works through his vices, though, he finds true connection with Rita, played by Andie MacDowell. Yet, she rejects all his advances, even after learning that the day will just reset.

And then it happens—the day everything changes.

In the beginning, Phil interprets this time loop as a curse. He thinks it is keeping him from pursuing a better life, imprisoning him in a job that is beneath him. (You might say a *reality* he desperately wants to bend.) He's been dying to leave, trying anything and everything to escape his circumstances. And then one day, Rita becomes the external catalyst that changes his lens: Maybe this isn't a curse but an opportunity. Maybe it's a blessing in disguise. If he really is immortal and can live the same day over and over again, the possibilities are endless.

Rather than continuing to bellyache about his situation, Phil sets out to improve himself and make the most of his time. He learns how to play piano, speak another language, and chisel ice sculptures. He gets to know everyone in the town, and because of his knowledge about the events of the day, he does what he can to make their lives better.

Through his newfound belief that the time loop is a blessing and through his good actions to make the town a better place to live, he realizes that he's finally happy, something he thought he could only be if he moved into a bigger reporting market.

Spoiler alert: The movie ends with the clock radio turning on and announcing that it's February 3. Throughout the entire film, Phil has kept trying to *do something different* to change his reality (behavior modification), when really, he had to change his beliefs first and the right actions would naturally follow, creating the reality he actually wanted. In other words, creating the right behavioral architecture was the key to his future.

Now of course, this is just a movie—which is both good and bad for you. Bad because *you* don't get to repeat the same day over and over again. Time will keep ticking on the reality you are currently living. And if you want to change, it's up to you to do so sooner rather than later. But it's also good because it illustrates (in a comedic way) that we *all* do have infinite possibilities in front of us—*if* we see them and choose to take action.

If you want to bend reality, you have to construct an entirely new cycle. You can't just change your actions without ever addressing your thoughts, and you can't choose new thoughts without ever taking new actions (in fact, as you'll see, this is almost an impossibility). Thoughts and actions are intrinsically linked, and work together to form the behavioral architecture that creates a new loop.

When people first encounter the Reality Cycle, it can seem like a series of big thoughts and actions that move clockwise in a circle. To some degree this is true: *If I want to create a new reality, I need to completely change everything about my life today. Think and do new things and abandon the old, right now.* But that's the willpower fallacy sneaking in. Master Benders know that change occurs slowly (even if we hate doing things slowly) over time through consistent micro-actions. To start the transformation, they craft a self-reinforcing cycle: **New Belief → Micro-Action → Emotional Reward → Evidence → Reinforced Belief.**

Go back and look at the Perception Emotion Imagination Exchange graphic. As you bring in your old (or maybe a better word is *existing*) perceptions and emotions, they can't help but be transformed by the actions you are taking in your new Reality Cycle. This expansion turns the flat Reality Cycle into something much more dynamic and expansive. As you act and unlock new perceptions, new emotions, and new imagination, you expand your world and bend your reality.

In 2008, when it felt like my whole world was crashing down around me, I needed a new reality *fast*. In my panic, I felt the pressure to make massive changes. I thought that was the only way I was going to save my family and my business. But it wasn't massive action that saved us; it was small changes and time. It was waking up to possibility thanks to my wife. This changed my perception of my circumstances. (Remember her line, "I don't know what to do, either, but I know the guy I married, I know who he is, and I'm not worried about it.")

I couldn't make a difference overnight. Yet over the following weeks and months, my team and I were able to create and execute a plan that saved all our bacon. (I trained myself to look past what my eyes could see—all of the challenges before me—and *imagine* a different, better, amazing future.) Every time the old beliefs crept into my mind, sowing seeds of doubt, I dug into the emotion of the moment my wife reminded me of who I was and what I'd done. From that emotion, I challenged the doubt and fear and continued taking the actions necessary to change the situation.

Then, one morning, it was all over. We'd come out the other side.

Don't wait for big action. Don't wait for confidence to come. Don't wait for permission. Don't even wait for clarity. Instead, *act* immediately, even if the action is small, because the purpose of the action isn't the outcome as much as it is about *proof*. Proof appears when the action starts. Proof signals to the brain: "This belief isn't fantasy—it's functional." Once evidenced, the behavior becomes easier, the identity forms, and reality begins to take shape.

Proof is going to the gym on Day 8 even if you were disappointed by Day 7, and finding out you can lift that weight three reps more than you could yesterday.

Proof is receiving thanks for your keynote (the first one you've ever given) and being asked to come back.

Proof is getting your first referral client because you brought so much value to someone else's experience.

Proof always starts out small, but quickly compounds into something bigger, something reality-changing.

In other words, once the brain receives evidence that a new behavior supports survival, identity, or progress, it adopts the behavior more readily. When behavior becomes easier, it becomes familiar, and we already know the brain is wired for familiarity and comfort.

Behavior is the bridge between belief and reality.

Knowing that you're getting stronger makes it easier to wake up for the gym on Day 9.

Knowing that you can, in fact, give a compelling keynote makes you eager to accept the next invitation.

Knowing that you can help someone change their life (you're not an imposter after all!) makes it exciting to start work with a new client.

So how do Benders build that bridge? Behavioral architecture!

THE FOUR STAGES OF BEHAVIORAL ARCHITECTURE

The Four Stages of Behavioral Architecture are not about willpower; they're about intentional, focused change on thoughts and actions, which when aligned, become a self-renewing cycle. This is how the intangible becomes inevitable.

These are four stages Benders use to create belief-driven behavior transformation:

- **Rewriting** the belief that drives the behavior
- **Installing** micro-behaviors that align with the new belief
- **Reinforcing** the emotional reward
- **Repeating** until it becomes your identity

Willpower is a finite resource. By definition, willpower is only meant to last for a short while. But bending reality is all about creating a whole new way of living. It takes time and a deep commitment—it's playing the long game—and that's why we've been laying the foundation for the past four chapters. But just because it's a long game doesn't mean it can't be broken up into smaller steps to make it achievable.

Everything I've asked you to do in the previous chapters has established a firm foundation for your behavioral architecture. Imagination and vision tap into future-back thinking and begin the work of shifting identity; thoughts create the mindset required to support the new identity and enable new action; actions generate the proof that gives life to the imagined future, solidifies the vision, reinforces the mindset, and shapes the new identity.

If this is your first time bending, your newly created imagined future and newly shifted thoughts probably still feel like a fresh, stiff pair of blue jeans. But I promise, if you keep with it, the edges of discomfort will soften and eventually fit like a glove. And when taken one stage at a time, what once may have appeared daunting and overwhelming will become invigorating and exciting.

Behavior follows belief like a shadow.

STAGE 1: Rewrite the Belief That Drives the Behavior

All behavior is belief in motion—the key is those beliefs are often deeply encoded and running by default in the background. So the old belief, "I'm not creative," leads to more of the same old behavior: avoiding brainstorming, not sharing ideas.

The new belief, "My imagination is a powerful tool," leads to more of the new behavior that creates a new reality: contributing, experimenting, exploring possibilities.

Behavior follows belief like a shadow. Until belief changes, behavior cannot. If you find yourself stuck in a behavior you don't like or that you know isn't building your new reality, look for the belief underneath. Recognize what emotion is driving you in that moment. Then, it's time to write a new script. *What would the person you are becoming believe in this moment? How would they act on that belief?* Sometimes the scripts that guide our actions are so deeply embedded that it takes work to get them out of your head and onto the page where you can see them for what they are—old wiring that holds you back.

STAGE 2: Install Micro-Behaviors That Align with the New Belief

Micro-behaviors are small, consistent actions that validate the new belief without alarming the brain. It's like taking your new belief for a test drive. If the new belief is, "I am a courageous leader," a micro-behavior might be to:

- Speak up once in a meeting
- Ask one difficult question
- Engage in one productive debate

Micro-behaviors bypass resistance and dodge the brain's defenses. They don't trigger the emotional alarms that big actions activate, and they create evidence for the brain. When you stack up enough of these micro-behaviors, guess what happens? New perceptions, new emotions, new imagination for a new future. All of this changes how you see yourself and the new reality you are creating.

STAGE 3: Reinforce the Emotional Reward

Every action creates an emotional outcome. Benders don't let these emotions go to waste; they capture them and use them to fuel their Reality Cycle. So when you take a micro-behavior that leads to a feeling of pride, or relief, or confidence, you capture that!

Benders don't ignore these emotions; they embrace them and magnify them. They stop and acknowledge them: "That felt good because it aligned with who I'm becoming." This emotional reinforcement strengthens the belief that the new behavior is not only possible but beneficial.

It's okay to savor these emotions. Actually, it's *critical* that you do this because these new emotions have the power to crowd out the old ones that hold you back. Tap into them early and often.

STAGE 4: Repeat Until It Becomes Identity

The brain loves repetition. It trusts repetition and it *learns* through repetition. (Remember learning your ABCs or multiplication tables, or all the words to "Gimme Three Steps" by Lynyrd Skynyrd blaring on the radio in your '76 Camaro with the T-Tops out? …sorry, that last one might have just been me.) When you repeat micro-behaviors, they eventually become familiar and then become the new normal. They no longer require intentional effort or conscious decision. This is how behaviors become identity and identity becomes reality. Once a behavior is embedded, momentum works *for* you instead of against you.

THINK, SEE, BELIEVE

As we move into the last phase of the bending process, I want to address a specific obstacle, one that every Bender will face at some point: What if you imagine the vision, create the new mindset, think the thoughts, and do the actions, but don't get the results you want?

Check your lens. It may be that there is a different perspective you need to consider. Benders view setbacks as setups. So if you're not experiencing the outcomes you expected, challenge how you're interpreting the results. Maybe you need a new lens altogether to see new possibilities that wouldn't have revealed themselves unless you achieved outcomes that didn't quite align with your desired outcomes.

We'll dive more into this story in the next chapter, but when I was trying to reinvent myself after the financial collapse, I started a journey of applying for jobs to pay the bills. I say "journey" because I received one denial after another. If I had a dollar for every "no" I heard that year, I would've easily been able to pay my bills! But throughout the interview process, people kept telling me that I should be a business consultant.

I'd never thought about consulting. Even with all my experience, I didn't think anyone would want to hire me to tell them how to run their business better. Who was I, anyhow? Yet the more I heard it, I decided to adjust my lens and imagine what it might look like. I began to perceive how valuable my expertise was and how unusual my experience was. I'd worked in four different industries at that point.

The more I thought about it, the more I could *see* myself as a consultant.

I began to bend my mind around the idea of that new reality and take small actions in that direction.

In the beginning, I couldn't get any traction with my consulting business, but several people told me that if I could teach what I knew, and help leaders become better through sharing my knowledge, I might be on to something. So I adjusted my lens again and approached someone I knew in the leadership training space. That led to becoming a trainer of leadership, which led to coaching leadership, which then led to keynote speaking on the subject of leadership, and so on to developing new training content for corporate workshops and licensing that content.

Eventually I also started writing books about leadership and business culture. But *none* of this would've happened had I not learned to adjust my lens when I heard the call of adjacent possible opportunities. (More on that in Chapter 8.)

As I learned, this is where you mold your new lens and see—maybe for the first time—that you're not at the mercy of your life. You're the creator of your reality.

Outcomes are not conclusions. They are feedback.

(RE)EVALUATE OUTCOMES

homas Edison was not the first person to invent the electric lightbulb. British inventors first had success with the arc lamp back in 1835. However, the arc lamp was too bright to use inside a house, so it was mainly confined to street and outdoor lighting, warehouses, and other large spaces. But this opened the door to the possibility of electric indoor light—a safer, cleaner, and more convenient alternative to gas. The competition was on. Who would be the first to make it practical?

Edison opened his Menlo Park, New Jersey laboratory in 1876 and started tinkering with incandescent lightbulbs two years later. The key to making electric lighting accessible for the masses was the filament. He needed something with high resistance, that was long-lasting, and not terribly expensive. After months of experimentation, in late 1878, he demonstrated his innovative platinum filament incandescent lightbulb, which was decidedly an improvement on the arc lamp … except it could only last about an hour before the platinum filament melted.[17]

Being a bit of a showman, however, Edison talked a big game, claiming he would light up all of lower Manhattan, and it worked. He received the financial backing to establish the Edison Electric Light Company in October 1878.[18]

With the pressure mounting, it was back to the drawing board. Edison and his team of inventors and scientists had no choice but to invent a truly lasting incandescent lightbulb—and fast.

From 1878 to 1880, Edison and crew worked through more than three thousand theories and six thousand types of filaments on their way to lighting Manhattan.[19, 20] If those numbers don't floor you, here's an overview of the process: choose a fibrous substance, like hickory; cut the material; plane it down to make it small enough to fit into the brackets of a lightbulb; carbonize it. I haven't even mentioned the other steps of this process, which include having someone blow the glass for the lightbulbs, build the mount, insert the insulation, etc. Can you imagine working for hours and hours to create *one* bulb, just to have it either not work or burn out as soon as the voltage flowed through the filament?

And Edison wasn't just developing the incandescent bulb at that time. He was also experimenting with commercial lighting schemes, electric railroads, and more. As a rabid inventor (dare I say, Reality Bender?) he was *constantly* trying things that didn't work.

Finally, in October 1879, with over 380 patents on lightbulbs, Edison and team found the right material to make electrical lighting in the home possible: bamboo. A carbonized bamboo filament could burn for over 1,200 hours and was cheap enough to produce for the average consumer to have electrical lighting. By late January 1880, he'd received the patent, and his lights and lighting schemes began entering public spaces.

When the average person fails once, they'll usually get back up and try again. They might even fail a few times and still try again. But imagine doing that fifty times, one hundred times, five hundred times.

How many times would it have taken you to give up making a better incandescent lightbulb?

What's even crazier to think about is that Edison was constantly "failing." Nothing is ever perfect the first time it's invented. It takes an incredible amount of experimentation.

One of the more famous quotes about Edison and his perspectives on experimentation came from a story that his assistant, Walter Mallory, shared and that was reprinted in the 1911 biography, *The Boy's Life of Edison*. The two had been working on a project, and Mallory was discouraged because the first nine thousand or so experiments hadn't worked. (Literally around nine thousand, per Mallory.) Edison is said to have responded, "Results!

Why, man, I have gotten a lot of results! I have found several thousand things that won't work."[21]

If Edison had hit his first obstacle and stopped, we wouldn't know his name. He'd be just another Joe who tried something once, didn't get the exact result he wanted, and so stopped trying. However, Edison knew that undesirable results weren't setbacks; they were setups for trying the next thing. They were clear answers about what *wouldn't* work, and they pointed him to new thoughts and theories he couldn't have had otherwise.

This brings us back to you and your journey to bending reality.

You've done everything right to this point. You've mined your emotional fuel, you've used your imagination, you've redesigned your Reality Cycle, and now you're on your way to new outcomes that will eventually remake the reality you inhabit. But understand that whatever ultimate, desired outcome you have in mind, your new reality will not come without its challenges and setbacks. To think otherwise would be naïve. However, the way you overcome those challenges, the way you push through those setbacks, will help you overcome the bias to interpret the setback as a loss, a defeat, a failure. It will help you overcome the desire to stop creating. (Remember that backwards inertia will always be exerting its pull—Reality Benders just won't let it.)

To be clear, this isn't about perseverance; this is about reframing the outcome. Look for the progress. Look for the setup, not the setback. What you find may open you to possible futures you could never imagine. Why? Because prior to that setback, you hadn't lived the conditions that allowed you to discover them in the first place.

THE WONDER OF THE ADJACENT POSSIBLE

Every Master Bender starts their bending journey with a specific vision for the future. As we discussed in Chapter 4, vision establishes the finish line, and imagination becomes the vehicle to get us there—it allows us to see ourselves in that new cycle. In visualizing that specific cycle, we set in motion everything that makes it possible, and we stay focused on creating it. Yet—and this may sound counterintuitive—while that one vision got us started, *hold it loosely.* There's a good reason for this open-handedness. Yes, it's completely possible to create that cycle exactly as imagined, but sometimes how we start is not where we end up. Sometimes we end up discovering cycles that we didn't have the foresight to imagine, but that we realize we'd rather have. This is the amazing part of bending reality. (Remember all those possible future realities? This is where those start to show up.)

It's like starting out with a vision of becoming a YouTube influencer and learning that what you really like about the process is creating the content. So rather than continuing to pursue your first vision (becoming a YouTube star), you pivot into the new, adjacent vision (content creator), and start a lucrative side hustle helping others decide what kind of content to create. You couldn't have skipped the chase for YouTube stardom and gone straight into content creation because you *didn't yet know* you liked creating content until you did it for your own videos.

I never thought I'd write a book. I never thought I'd get on stage and speak. I never thought I would be on a podcast. And I never thought I would do executive coaching—just to name a few impossible things I've done in my life. Those have been my adjacent visions; maybe not the first pursuit but just as powerful. And sometimes even more powerful than the first pursuit.

As a kid, I didn't have a vision for my life, and I didn't have goals other than not landing in jail. (Though, if I had, I wouldn't have been surprised.) But everything about my life and the way I saw myself changed the day my eighth-grade science teacher kept me after class.

Over the years, I had a number of other external catalysts, but the next big one was the 2008 financial collapse. Once things stacked up in my life that took away all other possibilities, all the outcomes I'd set out to achieve, there was nothing else to do but reinvent myself.

I've mentioned this in passing, but there is no specific time frame for bending, and it almost never happens instantaneously. More than anything, it requires establishing intentional thoughts and actions and pivoting based on outcomes you receive. But if you view it all through the Edison lens, *"I've found one more thing that doesn't work,"* you can overcome the interpretation bias that makes a gift pony into a burden. And that's exactly what I had to do to keep doing, because it took about two years of fighting battles all the way until I felt like that was all behind me. By the end of it, I was broke but free.

The economy still had not recovered, so going back into real estate development or anything related to it was impossible. So I had to rely on my adjacent visions, my adjacent possibles. The question was where to start. I was a serial entrepreneur, and I knew a little bit about business, which led me to found a men's support group called Man². We worked with men like me and my colleagues who'd lost their identity through this crisis, and helped them detach their identity from what felt like an unrecoverable tragedy.

Just to add some context, while we were all affected by this in some way: Unless you were in real estate development or something related, it's hard to understand how devastating a loss this was. The people we worked with were going out of business, like my friends and I had. Everyone was losing their jobs and couldn't support their families. Many had mountains of debt. I knew several people who just never recovered. It was literally a matter of life or death.

In my own mind, and then later at Man^2, I kept asking, "What's the next possibility?"

My goal at that point was simple: *How do I begin to create income again?*

As I ran the group, I circulated my resume, trying to get a job. But I hadn't worked for anyone else since I was twenty-seven. Now here I was, a middle-aged man trying to get a job. I was collecting rejections left and right. (Old Tom Edison would have been proud.) Either I didn't know enough about a specific field to be able to do it, or I was too experienced for the role that I'd applied for. One guy even told me, "You know, we'd love to hire you. You're perfect for the role, but you've been in business for yourself for so long that you'll only come here, work for a while, and then you'll go off and leave us."

I practically jumped over his desk, grabbed his collar, and begged, "Just give me a chance! Hire me! I need a paycheck. I'll stay as long as you want and do whatever you ask me to do!"

But nothing I did brought the outcomes I wanted, and every rejection seemed to chip away at the moorings that tied me to my past. The only vision I had was getting a job, and I was open to whatever possibility, adjacent or otherwise, would cover the cost of my mortgage and groceries. Also, maybe I was emotionally numb at that point or something else was happening, but each of those little defeats were so much less painful than the one I'd left behind that it was almost easy for me to pass through them. They didn't feel like obstacles or challenges as much as they were experiments. *Platinum filament burned out too fast? Okay, let's try a different one.*

Every "no" was one step closer to the right "yes," one I couldn't yet imagine.

Because of my business background, I decided to do some consulting work. I reached out to my network and let them know what I was doing. One of the people I reached out to was a guy who worked for one of my builder clients. My real estate company had done the sales and marketing for their homes. Over the years, we'd served as their advisors and tripled the size of their annual sales. After the real estate crash, he went back to work for a company he'd worked for right out of college. That company was in the leadership training and development business.

He called me with an opportunity.

"Hey, I'm working at a business leadership company, we train leaders. Why don't you join us? Bring your business flair into what we're doing over here?"

Like so many things in my life, I'd never led a training or developed courses before, but when you're trying to figure out how to buy pork and beans for dinner because that's all you can afford, you'll take anything. I also figured I could do it—I imagined myself doing it and the emotion it created *felt good*—so I accepted the opportunity.

I ended up facilitating training programs and putting a business spin on some of that company's existing content—something I never would have planned on doing because, well, I'd never done it before. But when push comes to shove, and perspectives change your lens, it's amazing how opportunities present themselves.

Whenever I mine the past now, I can clearly see how this future was an adjacent possibility all along. But I had to get hit over the head with the 2008 external catalyst in order to be open to it.

As life started getting better, I personally began shifting into an internal catalyst for myself. Working in the corporate training space sparked ideas (and a vision for a new reality) where I would create my own content to train business leaders to be more effective and authentic and to build dynamic organizational culture. I began sketching out the concepts for future workshops.

While I was developing this business content, though, something unexpected happened when my middle son began going through a tough time. He had been tagged as the "weird one" among his peers, and as a result, he was struggling with his identity. He didn't want to be who he was, but he didn't know how to be the version of himself that people would accept.

In his words, he just wanted to be "normal."

In response to his experience, I wrote a book called *Be Weird: How to Succeed in Life and Business Simply by Being You*. It's deeply personal to me because I wanted to encourage and empower him and others who may experience the judgment of others and feel the pull to abandon themselves to find acceptance. Even though it wasn't a commercial success, I still love it. It served its purpose in helping my son and I grow into new versions of ourselves.

Knowing that I could write a book gave me a boost of confidence, as well, and led me to turn my business content into my second book, *The 4 Dimensions of Culture: And the Leaders Who Shape Them*. This book is about building and leading a culture that wins in the marketplace. Of the two, *The 4 Dimensions of Culture* continues to be successful beyond anything I could've imagined. In fact, that content has been developed into additional workshops and digital resources—outcomes I couldn't have foreseen.

The sales of *Be Weird,* on the other hand, probably makes it seem like a failure. But that's only if the measurement of success is money. It's not. Writing that book gave me a new identity—

author—and deepened my relationship with my son. It was an absolutely, 100 percent necessary step because it was a work of passion that opened the door to new possibilities.

In this cycle of my life, all of these outcomes—facilitating training programs, developing business content, writing books— led to more exciting Reality Cycles that I couldn't have imagined back in 2008. I've since started a coaching business, am writing my third book (the one you're holding), and traveled all over this country and to eighteen others around the world giving keynote speeches and consulting with leaders in all sizes of business and in all kinds of industries. I've been in the restaurant business. I've worked in the entertainment business. I have many patents in the automotive industry from a business I started with a partner. Again, I don't say this to brag, but if I'd been locked into one specific outcome and had considered anything else to be a defeat, none of this would've happened. This kid from Mississippi who still has Mississippi mud between his toes never could have imagined or predicted all those possibilities.

I had to become someone new. I had to learn to bend reality.

I don't share my own story because I think I'm the greatest thing in the world, but I share all this in this book because I truly believe you can learn something from me. I share my experience because, as I reflect on my life to this point, I've discovered something that I'd like to help you put to intentional use in your own life to unlock *your own* unlimited possibilities and new reality.

That's the power of the Reality Cycle: It's not a framework to establish one specific outcome for your life—it's the beginning of a wild adventure.

LENS OF ADVENTURE

This book began with the parable of the farmer and his sons, a story about how our lenses affect our vision and interpretation of outcomes. While the majority of it has been about recognizing and understanding how the Reality Cycle works and how you can tap into that creative power to intentionally design a new cycle for yourself, every step along the way has subtly reshaped your lens. If you're the son who sees his pony as a burden, there is no cycle in which you don't see the manure first. But if you work the steps in the cycle to mold and reshape how you see the outcomes, eventually, the pony will be the greatest gift and the manure will just be something you have to shovel every once in a while, except now it won't ruin your day.

Mindset and leadership coach Brendan Harris posted a video on Instagram called "How to Win Every Time."[22] In this video, a girls' track team coach talks about one of his young runners. He'd worked with her for a few weeks, and at her first race, she came in last. She was sad and upset about her loss. His response: "You weren't last."

"Yes, I was," she replied.

"You were eighteen seconds," he said, and goes on to explain that he had previously marked her at nineteen seconds, and she smashed that. "This means it's your *lifetime best* performance. Your own personal record." Because of this small shift in mindset, this girl now defines winning as anything better than eighteen seconds, regardless of where she ends up in the pack.

Comparing yourself to others will almost always leave you feeling like you're falling behind. Comparing yourself to the you you are becoming (thinking future back)—*that's* where the magic happens. That's where perspective *shifts*. That's where reality *bends*.

Benders aren't tied to outcomes; they're open to possibilities.

In shifting how we interpret outcomes, from setbacks to setups, from failures to "several thousand things that won't work," we're not only creating a new cycle, we're also opening ourselves up to the adjacent possible. We're allowing ourselves to explore what's possible, things we never could have imagined. We're elevating our thought frequencies; we're living from belief-driven action. We're positively exploding with limitless potential. And no matter where we end up, it won't be a failure to achieve; it'll be a life worth living. It'll be an adventure.

Benders aren't tied to outcomes; they're open to possibilities. Unknown possibilities live within outcomes. It's just a matter of repositioning your lens and refining your interpretation of those outcomes. Sometimes those possibilities aren't obvious; sometimes they take a little work to uncover—like the second son, who was prepared to dig through as much manure as he had to in order to find the pony. You have to allow yourself to be open to the possibility that the most obvious outcome may not be *it*, even if it was your first vision, the one that got you started. It's all part of the adventure.

When I was around thirty years old, I started a technology company with a partner. He was telling me about some technology, which wasn't anything more than an engineering drawing at that point. I agreed to help him get it made. We eventually patented the technology for a continuously variable transmission for automotive use. At that time, no one knew about this or used it, but now it's all over the automotive industry. But back then, we couldn't sell it to anyone. I was going broke (again). I'd invested everything I had in that business.

Yet there was a president and CEO of a major car manufacturer making all this racket about how American industry had let the Japanese manufacturers take over the automotive market, and we needed to make America the automotive giant it used to be.

So I sat down and wrote him a letter. I said something to the effect of, "You rattle off about all this stuff. We've tried to get your engineers to take a look at our technology. You are suffering from NIH syndrome, Not Invented Here." (There were probably some other things in there I wouldn't repeat in polite company, but I went ahead and sent it off.)

About three weeks later, I got a phone call from an engineer from that car manufacturer.

"Mr. X has asked me to reach out to you," he said.

I almost hung up the phone because I didn't believe him. Good thing he convinced me otherwise.

My business partner and I scraped together the money to fly Eastern Airlines, the cheapest flights at the time, and went to speak with Mr. X in person.

He offered to buy the technology outright from us. It was a lot of money at the time. And it took everything I had to say no.

On the flight home, my partner and I looked at each other, and I said, "Did we just piss in our Post-Toasties?"

He responded, "I don't know, but you know what? If I'm going to go broke, I can't think of anybody I'd rather go broke with."

Not long after that, we did license the technology our company had designed. But if I'd interpreted those initial "no's" as the gospel, I wouldn't have written the letter. I wouldn't have flown out to meet with Mr. X himself. I would've lost everything. The list of never-would-haves goes on and on and on.

Instead, I kept experimenting and did something even 2026 Greg still thinks was bold. I ended up with an outcome different from the one I envisioned, but it wasn't a failure. Far from it. It made the next thing possible.

In my early years and at certain other points in my life, I either didn't know it was time for a new cycle or didn't try to change cycles *until* an external catalyst prompted me. It's completely fine to wait for something to tap you on the shoulder and say, "Hey, this is the sign. Get bending." But many times, we have glimpses of a new cycle, and for whatever reason, we ignore them and don't change until we absolutely must. In other words, we waste a lot of time that could be better spent.

The older I get, the more I value the ability to be my own internal catalyst. Instead of waiting to act when a new vision comes along, I now understand that the appearance of the new vision in and of itself *is the sign* that it's time to get to work. Otherwise, why would the vision show up? So instead of waiting around for something external, I get bending. I start living in the new cycle sooner and maximize the amount of adventure I experience and minimize (sometimes totally eliminate) the pain of an external catalyst. Because it can take a lot of pain to compel us to change.

When you follow the cycle in this book, you won't have to rely on the pain or wake-up call of an external catalyst to jumpstart your cycle transformation; you'll have the tools to be your own internal catalyst at any point. You will have the power to choose when and where to get bending.

And this is only the beginning. As I'll show you, once you understand and intentionally work the Reality Cycle, you can create the conditions that allow others to recreate their own cycles, to also live in alignment that unlocks *their* unlimited possibilities. That's where the true calling lies.

Breaking free from your past requires radical self-forgiveness. Reality Benders forgive themselves and move forward.

chapter nine

PAY IT FORWARD: THE TRUE MEASURE OF A REALITY BENDER

ou may have picked up this book thinking all of it was for you—that you were learning how to master your own Reality Cycle for your benefit. But I have something to confess: This was never about you.

Mastering your own cycle was never about you, and it was never about me, either. Becoming a Master Bender is and always has been about impacting others. Let me explain.

A Master Bender has not only learned how to master their own reality, they also apply that same process to help others bend *their* realities. They guide them through the process of reigniting the imagination, of envisioning a greater cycle, of reframing outcomes and consciously choosing their thoughts and actions. They become the external catalysts others need to live better lives.

They can't help it—it's just what Benders do.

Consider all the examples I've shared in this book—President Kennedy, Dr. Houboult, and the Apollo mission that finally landed a man on the moon; Tony Robbins and the millions of people he's affected over the past four decades; my eighth-grade science teacher Jane Moring; Dolly Parton; Eddie Murphy; Thomas Edison. While I used their stories to illustrate different parts of reality bending, they've all lived lives that *lifted others up.* Whether they inspired from afar or directly affected someone's life through mentoring, charity work, or relief aid, or in the case of Ms. Moring, counseling a young man on the edge, they've used their lives and their platforms for the benefit of others.

This book started out as a guide to wake you up to the Reality Cycle driving your life so that you can create the cycle you actually want. As we said in Chapter 8, the journey starts with the vision for a specific outcome, but the magic happens in opening up to the unknown possibilities that arise along the way.

Now we're taking it one step farther and one step deeper: To become a Master Bender, you must apply these concepts for the benefit and value and impact of others.

BECOMING WHO YOU WERE ALWAYS MEANT TO BE

To be a Master Bender means joining an elite group of people dedicated to adding value to others. Anyone is capable and everyone is called, but too many leave the call unanswered. We hear the words "lead" or "leader," and our minds often jump to becoming the head of an organization or managing groups of people. Then suddenly, the idea of being a Master Bender grows beyond what we think we can do.

> *It's too big a job for a normal person like me, we think. I don't have enough experience bending. I don't have enough knowledge. I sometimes stumble over obstacles, get bogged down by setbacks, and can't always be my own internal catalyst. If I can't do it for myself all the time, if I can't master it perfectly, then I'm probably not meant to influence others.*

So we don't.

In response to these thoughts, we shrink.

We limit ourselves. We limit our abilities. We limit our impact.

We go on improving and expanding our own lives and choose to ignore the call to mentor and guide others. Yet in choosing to not act, to not be an external catalyst for others, to not guide the people in our spheres of influence, we've not only made a decision that will impact our own lives, but we've also taken away the chance for others to become the best versions of themselves and in turn impact others within their sphere of influence. We've made both their realities and ours just a bit smaller.

Success fades.
Significance endures.

I don't want this to feel like a slap in the face, but I do want it to be a kick in the pants. I want you to have a great life. I want you to create the life you want to live. But I don't think you can sincerely do that without also making the lives of others better.

In fact, I'm going to say it's impossible.

I'm in my sixties now, and I've worked really hard for most of my life. I feel like I've earned the credibility to say this: No matter how many accolades you win, how much material wealth you amass, or how many businesses you've run, there comes a point when success in the traditional sense feels empty. Yes, you may have helped a lot of people along the way of your conventional success, but until you start *intentionally* investing in others, all of that "success" goes away eventually.

I've never gone to a funeral and heard someone say, "That John, he earned five million dollars in 1996. It inspired me." *No!* They say, "That John, he reached out to me when I was having a tough time and coached me through opening my first business. He was so kind and generous with his time, it inspired me to coach some of the younger associates in my office. I want to pay it forward because of him."

Success fades. Significance endures.

I'd rather live a life of significance than a life of success.

Bending always begins internally, but a bent reality that ends with you is not fully bent.

The good news is, I don't have to choose between the two. You don't, either. In fact, the two are very closely tied together. Success without significance is a reality that doesn't really exist. Success without significance creates a reality that is self-contained. It serves the individual, but it does not extend beyond them. It generates comfort, validation, and sometimes admiration—but it does not generate transformation. And transformation is the true mark of a Reality Bender.

Bending always begins internally, but a bent reality that ends with you is not fully bent. First, you learn to see differently. You regulate your emotions. You challenge inherited beliefs. You imagine new outcomes. You act in alignment. Your life changes. Yes, all of that. But the **cycle** was never meant to stop there.

The ultimate proof that you have mastered your own Reality Cycle is not how far you go—it's how many others begin to move because of you. When your clarity becomes a mirror for someone else, when your imagination gives others permission to dream bigger, when your emotional steadiness helps others regulate chaos, when your beliefs interrupt someone else's limitation loop—*that* is significance.

The ultimate proof that you have mastered your own Reality Cycle is not how far you go—it's how many others begin to move because of you.

For the Master Bender, impact is not a side effect of success. It is the outcome that success was meant to produce. This is why a life of pure achievement eventually feels hollow.

Achievement measures what you build. Significance measures what you awaken.

Achievement accumulates. Significance multiplies.

When you impact someone else's reality, you guide them to reframe their lens, reengage their imagination, and choose a higher cycle. When you do that, you create a ripple that extends beyond your reach. That ripple may move through families, teams, communities, or generations you will never meet. The reason significance outlasts success is because significance is not stored in titles, accounts, or accolades. It lives in people. You should always be asking yourself, "What's my ripple effect?"

That doesn't mean you need to be overly assertive. It does mean you need be intentional. It means recognizing your words, your presence, your questions, and your encouragement have weight. It means understanding that every interaction is an opportunity to either reinforce someone's existing reality or help them bend toward a better one.

Achievement measures what you build. Significance measures what you awaken. Achievement accumulates. Significance multiplies.

Having said this, I understand the allure of success. And traditional success has its place when you're young and pursuing your career and your dreams in life, when your fulfillment comes from your own accomplishments and the things you can achieve. Growing up as I did, I know what it feels like to live with insecurity and just want to know that I can afford a roof over my head and food on my table. Do that. In fact, pursue that with passion. Go after your dreams with all you have. But know that real fulfillment in life is almost always tied to the contributions we make to other people and how we can help them be more effective, more fulfilled, and live out *their* version of significance.

Being a Master Bender isn't necessarily about living a big life. Every person on this planet has a sphere of influence. It could be a sphere of one, could be twenty, a hundred, or yes, five thousand. It doesn't matter how big or small that sphere is. So the question you need to ask yourself is, *Are the people I encounter better because they crossed* my *path? Are they significantly impacted in a good way? Are they better versions of themselves because our paths crossed?*

Achieving a life of significance happens in the small moments of the day, in quiet and sometimes vulnerable conversations. It's helping your child reframe a setback into a setup. It's guiding your team through imaginative brainstorming and problem-solving. It's supporting someone through a tough time and opening their imagination to opportunities.

Becoming a Master Bender is the next natural step in the bending process. And like bending your own cycle, it starts with cultivating the right mindset.

THE PRIVILEGE OF THE CALL

The "life of significance" mindset separates the extraordinary from the average. The Master Bender graciously accepts the call to guide others, and sees it as a privilege. The average person knows they should guide others and that it's part of living a purposeful life, but with the wrong mindset, it can sometimes feel like a burden. It keeps them from doing other things, more important things. The Master Bender knows *it* is the most important thing, the task to be tended above all others. (One final time, you might want to read that again and underline it for good measure.)

The Master Bender knows it is the most important thing, the task to be tended above all others.

When you understand the importance of investing in others, especially those you've been entrusted to lead, your bending abilities become magnified. This goes all the way back to Chapter 2—your lens expands as you can suddenly see endless possibilities all around you through the lives you touch. The energy of your thoughts elevates yet again as you watch and experience others change their lives, and your joy grows. Your imagination ignites with bigger and brighter visions as you pursue greater impact. You suddenly feel electric. And the connections between all of humanity become clearer.

The call becomes very clear—to love others, to lift them up, to extract the best out of all of us.

None of this is to say we will do it perfectly every time. We won't. But we're not pursuing perfection; we're pursuing impact. In fact, the power of you is not perfection, it's your imperfections. Your imperfections are what make you unique and what endears you to others. When in doubt, go back to the beginning: What's your lens? Where's your heart? Is your vision clear? What's directing your thoughts?

If something feels out of alignment, figure out what it is. Then you can move forward.

This is about living a life of significance.. You're here for a reason, for a purpose, and for a season. *How* you live it is up to you.

———————

This project has been a journey for me. It has caused me to revisit my own Reality Cycles. I found myself doing more than explaining a framework. I was reliving decisions, reexamining motivations, reconciling parts of my past, and quietly reshaping the cycle I'm living right now. I was reminded that bending is never something you complete and move past. It's something you return to, again and again, with more honesty and self-examination each time.

You never truly get to the end of it … even at the end.

That shouldn't feel discouraging. If anything, it's the invitation. Growth doesn't have a finish line. Meaning doesn't arrive fully formed. If you ever reach a place that feels like the end, it's usually just life asking you to begin again, to see differently, to choose again, to bend anew—to create another new Reality Cycle to take you into the next phase of your life.

This work is not linear. It's a lifelong adventure. And I do mean *adventure*.

What surprised me most as I wrote was how humbling it was to look backward with clear eyes. Not just at the wins, but at the moments where I lived on autopilot. The times I let fear, comfort, or old beliefs quietly make my decisions while I told myself I was being "practical" or "responsible." Writing this book forced me to confront those moments—not with shame, but with clarity and grace.

There were chapters of my life when I looked successful by most outward measures, yet I felt internally disconnected from who I knew I was meant to become. I achieved goals. I crossed milestones. And still, there was a quiet tension, an awareness that achievement without alignment of purpose costs more than it gives. That realization didn't arrive all at once. It came slowly—through reflection, through relationships, through failure, and through grace.

Because there is a kind of success that looks impressive while you're living it, but doesn't survive the finish line.

It's the success that fills calendars but empties meaning.

The success that builds comfort but avoids contribution.

The success that answers the question *"What did I achieve?"* but never confronts *"Who was changed because I lived?"*

That kind of success isn't wrong. It's just incomplete.

If success does not eventually turn outward, if it does not mature into service, impact, and investment in others, it begins to hollow out. What once felt motivating slowly becomes maintenance. What once felt fulfilling now asks for more and gives less.

Significance is not the opposite of success. It is what success becomes when it matures.

That's where Reality Bending becomes more than personal growth. It becomes intentional living.

One of the most grounding questions I've learned to ask, one that reshaped how I see everything, is this: *How will this matter when I look back from the end of my life?*

When you allow the future to speak first, the present gets quieter.

When you allow the future to speak first, the present gets quieter. The noise fades. The pressure to chase what looks impressive loses its luster. What remains is surprisingly clear: people, purpose, contribution, love. Combine those and the result is significance!

This is what it means to live life from the future back. Borrow wisdom from the finish line and let it shape how you live today. To stop building a life around things that won't survive reflection.

If there's one thing I want you to understand, it's this: I didn't write this book from a place of mastery. I wrote it from a place of practice. I am still bending. Still noticing when my lens narrows. Still catching myself when old emotional patterns try to reclaim control. Still learning to choose imagination over fear, intention over drift, courage over comfort. In fact, as I worked on this project with my writing team, they served as "master benders" to me. Their contribution to this project extended into my reality cycle and gave me the courage to be vulnerable, reflect on unresolved things in my past, and to imagine much more than I would without them.

And that's the point.

Reality Bending isn't about having it all figured out. It's about being awake. Awake to the stories you're telling yourself. Awake to the emotions driving your decisions. Awake to the beliefs shaping both your limits and your possibilities.

If this book has done its job, it hasn't given you answers. It has given you *awareness*. It hasn't handed you certainty. It has invited you into responsibility: the responsibility to choose your lens, to tend your inner world, to imagine more for your life, and then to act in alignment with that imagination.

But I want to challenge you here, at the end.

Don't let this be a good book you enjoyed or a set of ideas you agreed with. Don't let it sit neatly on a shelf while your life continues unchanged. If nothing shifts—if no belief is questioned, no habit disrupted, no conversation approached differently—then this was just information. And information without transformation is wasted.

Action is what drives transformation.

So here's the invitation: Begin again. Today. With one small, intentional choice. One reframed story. One courageous conversation. One moment where you refuse to default to who you've been and instead act like who you're becoming.

And as you do, don't keep it to yourself.

Help someone else see what you now see. Help them imagine what they haven't dared to imagine yet. Help them believe change is possible because you are living proof that it is. That is how success becomes significance.

So I'll leave you with the question I continue to ask myself:

If success were taken away, would the way I live still matter?

If the answer is yes, you are living a life of significance.

If the answer is no, the work isn't finished yet.

That's not a condemnation. It's an invitation.

I believe you were never meant to live a small, unconscious life. I believe you were meant to shape reality; first within yourself, then far beyond you. I believe the world is quietly waiting for more people willing to live awake, aligned, intentional, and future-back.

This is not the end of the journey.

It's the moment you decide to bend ... on purpose.

*Human potential
rises on the energy
of emotion.*

hile I hope this book has helped you begin to identify and embrace your ability to bend to your reality, I understand that it isn't as easy as read, then execute. Sometimes we need specific actionable assessments and exercises. So as a coach, your personal Bender Coach, I've put together these appendices that dive deeper into your bending journey. You may not need or want to take every assessment and do every exercise. That's okay. Use only what you need.

- If you're interested in exercises that target different aspects of Reality Bending, go to **Appendix A: Bending in Real Time**. These are designed to help you tap into the power of your emotions, re-ignite your imagination, and create a vision for your new Cycle that gets you excited to bend.

- If you'd like to assess your Bender Leader skills as they are currently, jump to **Appendix B: The BendStyle Profile (Life Edition)**. This assessment will pinpoint your abilities to make space for new ideas, how you work with emotion, and your aptitude for turning intentions into results. It also includes a quick analysis of how well you're leading the Reality Cycle.

- As I've spent the latter half of my career working with business leaders, I had to include a chapter of practical application for bending in the workplace. If you're in business and interested in how you can apply Reality Bending in the office, read **Appendix C: Bending in Business.**

After reading Appendix C, consider taking the assessment in **Appendix D: The BendStyle Profile (Business Edition)** to determine what bending characteristics you already apply at work and where you have room for growth.

Finally, **Appendix E: The Six BendStyle Types (all-in-one profiles)** details each of the six BendStyle Types identified in the BendStyle Profile assessment. You will learn about your specific bending strengths, pitfalls, tips for leaning into your BendStyle and more.

BENDING IN REAL TIME

ou've learned what it takes to bend your reality. Now I'm going to challenge you to put it into practice.

I've designed the following exercises to help you reignite your imagination and vision, create your emotional anchor, shift your thoughts and actions, and reinterpret your outcomes in order to bend your reality. Consider this additional coaching to help you on your path to becoming a Master Bender. In fact, I've used all of these exercises in my one-on-one coaching or group training sessions, and I've practiced them at different points in my own life.

I would also encourage you to dedicate a notebook to these exercises and write out your answers by hand. Take time to think about them. Take time to reflect. Periodically revisit your answers and work through the exercises again.

You don't have to do every single one, but I would suggest following the order set out in this Appendix—for example, maybe you like the first and third exercises but not the second. Don't skip ahead and do the third exercise first and then return to the first. Do them in this order, just skip the second one. The reason for this is that these exercises build on each other and line up with the order of the Reality Cycle bending process.

In every cycle, you will become a new version of yourself, a new possible you. You'll have different and valuable thoughts and feelings about the experience of your life. You'll have learned new lessons, done new things. All of it becomes the story of your life. And from where I'm standing right now, it's always incredible to go back and see who you've been and how you've changed. Then, if you ever doubt your status as a Master Bender, you'll see the proof, there on the page in black and white, and it'll give you the strength and courage to keep bending.

FLIP YOUR SCRIPT

In this first exercise, we're going to work on understanding your lens.

Don't kid yourself: Most performance reviews, self-improvement plans, and even parenting tactics are built around evaluating gaps and focusing on what's missing—remember the research team from Chapter 2? That's a prime example. That's why most teams, families, and individuals never break the cycle—they're addicted to deficit thinking.

You want out of that cycle? You have to see it to change it. Start by asking yourself, ***What reality am I scanning for? Whose script am I following?***

Start Here:

- Notice today: Are you looking for the goodness or benefit in a given situation, or are you complaining about an opportunity? Thinking back to the farmer and his sons: Are you shoveling for the hidden pony, or inventing reasons to resent the perfectly good horse in your stall?

- Ask someone you trust what lens they see you using—don't justify, just listen.

- This week, catch yourself using deficit language ("not enough," "always behind")—and then flip it. What's the one thing working? Grab it and magnify it.

Your reality is not a given. Your lens is not a sentence. **The future bends when you do.**

NEGATIVE LENS SCAN

In Chapter 2, we talked about the four lenses that can keep us trapped in negative Reality Cycles. After reading that section, you may have already identified your natural tendencies towards resistance, limiting, changing, or perfection. However, if you'd like to explore those ideas further, this assessment can help you pinpoint a few of the specific moments these lenses come into play in your life. Answer **Yes** or **No** to each question. Count **Yes** answers per lens type.

Resistor: *"I thrive in crisis."*

		YES	NO
1	DO I FEEL MOST USEFUL WHEN THINGS ARE BREAKING?	☐	☐
2	HAVE I EVER CREATED URGENCY TO JUSTIFY MY ROLE OR ACTION?	☐	☐
3	DO CALM PERIODS MAKE ME ANXIOUS OR BORED?	☐	☐
4	DO PEOPLE SAY, "WHEN IT HITS THE FAN, WE CALL YOU"?	☐	☐
5	WOULD I RATHER FIX FIVE FIRES THAN PREVENT ONE?	☐	☐

SCORE: ☐ / 5

Negative Impact: Seeking out or creating chaos because it feels like progress.

Reality Bender Antidote: Refocus. Remind yourself of what you want to achieve. With that clear in your mind, work backwards to determine what actions you need to take to get that outcome and what thoughts and mindsets you need to initiate those actions in order to create the right lens.

Limiter: "Good is good enough. Don't rock the boat."

		YES	NO
1	DO I PULL THE PLUG WHEN MOMENTUM GETS TOO STRONG?	☐	☐
2	HAVE I KILLED A BOLD IDEA TO PROTECT MYSELF?	☐	☐
3	DO I CELEBRATE CONSISTENCY OVER BREAKTHROUGHS?	☐	☐
4	DOES GROWTH OR GOING BIGGER FEEL RECKLESS OR IRRESPONSIBLE?	☐	☐
5	DO I SECRETLY FEAR OUTGROWING MY CYCLE?	☐	☐

SCORE: ☐ / 5

Negative Impact: Creating a ceiling to growth and curtailing what you believe you deserve.

Reality Bender Antidote: Challenge those limiting beliefs to choose to act differently. Recognize the limits you put on yourself, and identify the behaviors that sabotage your happiness and growth. Then see yourself as someone who deserves more than you're allowing, even if it feels forced to begin with. It will feel uncomfortable before it becomes natural.

Change Agent: *"New direction, new energy … again."*

		YES	NO
1	HAVE I LAUNCHED THREE OR MORE "PIVOTS" IN THE LAST YEAR?	☐	☐
2	DO I GET BORED THREE MONTHS INTO ANY PROJECT OR CYCLE?	☐	☐
3	DO PEOPLE ROLL THEIR EYES WHEN I TALK ABOUT MY NEXT NEW IDEA?	☐	☐
4	ARE MY FAMILY AND FRIENDS EXHAUSTED FROM MY CONSTANT REINVENTION?	☐	☐
5	DO I ABANDON OPPORTUNITIES BEFORE THEY'RE PROVEN?	☐	☐

SCORE: ☐ / 5

Negative Impact: Never allowing yourself to go deeper or fully developing in something before moving on; can't finish what you've started.

Reality Bender Antidote: Pinpoint the origins of your desire to correct, continuously improve, and change. Ask yourself, "Why am I uncomfortable with being who I am right now? Why can't I accept something as it is?" Accepting who you are isn't the same as being complacent with your life. You don't have to be perfect to have impact, get your point across, or be relevant—in fact, none of the people you admire, including your mentors, are perfect. But they have found a way to do their best and keep moving forward. So choose your reality, and like the Resistor, outline the steps you need to take, and just take them.

Perfectionist: *"It's not ready. One more tweak..."*

		YES	NO
1	DO I DELAY FINISHING SOMETHING FOR "JUST ONE MORE TWEAK"?	☐	☐
2	DO I REDO SOMETHING MULTIPLE TIMES?	☐	☐
3	DO I ZOOM IN 400 PERCENT TO FIX TINY "PROBLEMS" THAT DON'T HAVE ANY REAL IMPACT ON THE OVERALL PICTURE?	☐	☐

4   DOES "GOOD ENOUGH" FEEL LIKE FAILURE?   ☐ ☐

5   DO OTHER PEOPLE WAIT ON ME TO MOVE FORWARD IN A SITUATION OR PROJECT?   ☐ ☐

SCORE: ☐ / 5

Negative Impact: Stuck in a self-defeating cycle of delay driven by fear of failure. Constantly seeking flawless conditions before moving forward.

Reality Bender Antidote: Accept that imperfection is a part of growth and advancement. Progress happens through action, not perfect execution, and waiting for the "perfect" moment only prolongs inaction and fuels frustration. Accepting mistakes and uncertainties as part of the journey allows you to view setbacks as learning rather than personal failures. Eliminating unrealistic standards opens the door to a healthier Reality Cycle, inviting momentum and confidence to build with each step forward.

Your Lens Diagnosis

HIGHEST SCORE: (LIST TYPE) ______________________________

SCORE: ☐ / 5

SCORE	RISK OF CYCLE STAGNATION
0–1	MINIMAL
2–3	EMERGING
4–5	DOMINANT—YOU ARE STUCK IN THIS LOOP.

Your Seven-Day Bend Plan

MY DOMINANT LENS TRAIT: ______________________________

MY WEAKEST–LINK MOMENT: ______________________________

ONE EXPERIMENT I'LL RUN THIS WEEK OR ONE THING I'LL DO

DIFFERENTLY: ______________________________

WHO I'LL TELL: ______________________________

SUCCESS METRIC: ______________________________

WHO ARE YOU?

The Reality Cycle can keep you locked in place or set you free. It can justify everything that goes wrong or it can launch you into the life your imagination creates. But the first step is becoming aware of the cycle you're living in: Was it created from an outdated lens? Or was it the culmination of your intentional thoughts and actions? Either way, to make a new Reality Cycle, you have to recognize your embedded beliefs and behaviors if you want to change them.

How? With some mindfulness.

Start by asking yourself "Why?" every chance you get. It might sound excessive, but it will begin the process of self-revelation that will lead to discovering your embedded beliefs. And it's the beliefs, the embedded thoughts, that we need to change in order to bend your reality.

In practice, it looks like this:

You pour yourself a cup of coffee and automatically grab the creamer out of the refrigerator. STOP! Ask yourself, *Why do I always put creamer in my coffee? Do I even like it?*

You might answer, *No, I don't think I do, and my dentist mentioned I was getting a cavity. But my parents always put creamer in their coffee.*

Why did I start putting it in mine?

Because I began drinking coffee kind of young, and I didn't like the bitterness.

Why did I start drinking it young?

I had a job in high school, which meant I didn't begin studying until late at night. I never had enough sleep.

Why did I work so hard?

I didn't want to be a financial burden on my family and I wanted to earn a scholarship to a good college.

Why did I want the scholarship?

My parents didn't go to school, and they often struggled to find good work. They always told me that education was the key to a good life.

Why did they think education was the key to a good life?

Because the people running the businesses that employed them often had college degrees, and I suppose they wanted me to have an easier life than they did.

Do you?

I guess so. I don't struggle to pay my bills, and I'm one of the people in the office, not on the factory floor.

Do you like creamer?

No, not really. It's too sweet.

Why don't you skip it this time and see what happens?

Yeah, let's try something new.

Through that process, you just learned about the connection between your food choices, your upbringing, and your embedded beliefs about living a good life. As a result, you were able to slow down in the moment and consciously choose a different thought and action. It might not always go so deep, but then again, it might. No matter what, you're learning valuable information about your embedded beliefs and behaviors.

The next time you unconsciously act, or the next time a thought pops into your head, ask, *What is my thinking here? What drove me to do X?* Or *Why do I think X about Y?*

After you answer, continue drilling down with the following questions:

- Why do I think that way?

- What causes me to think that way?

What needs to change in my thinking to realign my lens with my imagination rather than the past?

If I *thought* differently, what would I *see* differently?

If I *saw* things differently, how would I *act* differently?

If I *acted* differently, how might my life be different?

You can't predict the future, but you can imagine it and create it one intentional choice at a time. Every time you make a different choice, you break up the familiar, outdated neural circuitry holding you back from getting to the next level and building your new Reality Cycle.

Every time you choose a new interpretation of an outcome, you reinforce the foundation of your new Reality Cycle. It will take time and effort for this overhaul to manifest completely, but the change necessary to create and sustain it occurs the very moment you think differently, see differently, and choose differently.

You have the power to make a different choice. You have the power to change your lens. You have the power to bend your reality.

MINING YOUR PAST

There are two techniques I've used and recommended to mine the past. One is simply journaling. Some of my clients enjoy sitting down with the purpose of writing about past triumphs and trials with an eye for discovering what emotions pulled them through. If you like journaling, please do this. Sit down and examine your proudest triumphs and your hardest trials.

- How did you pull through each situation?

- Was there a person cheering you on or counseling you in some way?

- What thoughts and feelings resulted, and how did they affect your behavior?

- How did these moments change you and your future actions? (Might be a similar answer to the question above.)

- How can you reinterpret these times through the lens of appreciation? What did they ultimately do for you?

If you don't like journaling or just generally find self-probing activities difficult, here's an alternative: write a letter to your past self.

I was coaching someone the other day, and we were talking about all the things in this man's life. He's lived a very rich life; it could be a novel. But he was trying to put it all together into who he was today, so I issued him a challenge: Write a letter to your younger self to encourage that version of you or help him/ her understand the value of the journey they're on. Don't tell them to change any decisions or anything like that; you're just trying to cultivate a sense of appreciation and gratitude for the tough things they're experiencing, and helping them see the purpose in the pain. You're reframing the setbacks as setups.

I never ask my clients to do something I haven't done myself, so I also wrote a letter to my younger self. I started talking to my younger self as someone I am proud of, someone that has created this wiser, better me, and I wanted to encourage him. I said,

Dear Younger Me,

You don't know it yet, but every choice you're making, the ones that thrill you, the ones that haunt you, and even the ones that leave you broken, are all part of something extraordinary.

The failures you feel so deeply, the pain you sometimes think will never pass, the rejection that stings like fire, they are not the end. They are what is shaping you into the person you're destined to become. One day, you'll see that the rejection was simply redirection. The struggles were never wasted; they were a training ground for strength. The setbacks weren't punishment; they were part of the setup for something bigger, better, and far more beautiful than you can imagine right now.

You'll discover that life was never happening to you. It was happening for you. Every trial, every triumph, every tear, and every laugh woven together is constructing a life that is rich, meaningful, and full of purpose.

Younger me, I want you to be proud: proud of the risks you took, proud of the lessons you learned, proud of the contribution you made to the man I am today. Because of you, I am wiser. Because of you, I am stronger. Because of you, I live with a deeper gratitude for every moment, every relationship, and every breath of this beautiful life journey.

Thank you for not giving up when it would have been easier to quit. Thank you for the courage to keep walking when the road was steep.

As you write, think about how your past has molded you. You know my story about the 2008 real estate meltdown. Do you think I would have chosen to take that journey? Of course not. But when

I look back on it, I can honestly say this with all conviction: If God Himself said, "Hey, I'll spare you from that, you don't have to go through that," I would say, "No, let's leave that one in place," because I like the older self that is a byproduct of that experience.

In mining the past, in reexamining and reinterpreting what's shaped our lives, we're not only creating the emotional anchor we need to move forward, we're also further breaking down any negative lens we might have. In changing our opinion of the past, we're changing our perspective/perception and raising the energy of our thoughts and emotions.

Going back to Chapter 1, where we talked about the energy of our thoughts and the Laws of Attraction, when we move from a lower state of energy to a higher state through reinterpretation and introduce appreciation and gratitude where there was pain, we're aligning the energy of thoughts and emotions. And when those two energies are aligned, just as the connection between imagination and emotion, the reality cycle comes to life.

One more thing I'd like you to do before leaving this exercise is reflect on the following questions I posed in the chapter:

- How do I need to think differently than I'm thinking right now to bring that reality to life?

- What do I need to do differently than I'm doing now?

- What do I already know from past experience that can help me believe this new reality is possible?

- What do I already know from my past experience that is getting in the way of my new reality?

- What emotion will I feel when I arrive there—and what emotion can I remember from my past that connects me to that feeling now?

IMAGINE THE NEXT POSSIBLE

Time to reignite your imagination. We want to imagine every detail about that future with an open mind. We're no longer thinking about what is and isn't possible *because it's all possible.* It's just a matter of which possible you want right now.

For example, say you want to be the next Tony Robbins—not Tony himself, but *your* version. In that vision, you will be speaking to tens of thousands of people from a stage. What are the details? What does it feel like? Are you nervous? Excited? Who are you in this reality? What are you wearing? What can you hear from backstage? When you step out onto the stage, are the lights hot? Are they blinding? Who can you see in the front row? What's the hands-free microphone headset sitting on your ear feel like? Or do you prefer the weight of a wireless microphone in your hand? Does your voice boom back into your ears from the speakers? And so on.

Close your eyes and give your mind permission to imagine your new Reality Cycle. Think about it for several minutes before you start writing out every detail. And don't just type it—write it out longhand, with a pen or pencil and a piece of paper. (I won't go into the science here, but there's a powerful mind-body connection when we write by hand rather than typing on screen, and we're all about mind-body connections when creating a new Reality Cycle.)

Once you've written out everything you can see, taste, feel, and hear about this new Reality Cycle and about the new version of you in that cycle, move into the next exercise, where we'll dive into the next version of you.

THE IDENTITY BREAKOUT

Bending your Reality requires a series of transformations. Reality Benders act unconventionally. The difference between Reality Benders and everyone else isn't talent, IQ, or grit; it's origin: Reality Benders act from their future identity, not their current one. They act as if the future version of themselves is already at work in their choices.

Too many people behave according to old stories, emotional memory, and comfort patterns. This leads to cycle stagnation. If you want to become an effective Bender, you need an unconventional approach. You need to behave from a chosen identity, designed beliefs, and future-back thinking.Your behavior can't be random, reactive, or accidental. It has to be designed and constructed.

This next reflection may look short, but the repetition of it, the work without the immediate evidence of manifestation, is the key.

1. Write the identity you've been living because it feels familiar.

2. Write the identity your future Reality Cycle demands.

3. List three familiar thoughts that keep you small.

4. Replace each with a **future-back** thought your new identity would think.

5. Take one action today that breaks the familiarity pattern.*

Repeat for thirty days. You will feel yourself evolving in real time.

> * *As you work through these prompts, consider listing out what specific action you will take every day—and even the time each day you'll complete it, if you need additional accountability. You might even tell a trusted friend or advisor about it and have them check in with you every day, "Did you do X today?"*

CONSTRUCTING THE FUTURE

You can't do the same thing over and again and create a different cycle. To build something new, you must *do* something new.

But what new? How should you change your actions to bring about the vision of your next cycle? There are a million different things you could do right now, and they would all change what happens next. Yet only specific actions will lead to the outcomes you want. Use your vision and new identity to guide what happens next. What's the next right thing?

Depending on the size of your vision, there may be many phases to building out your next cycle. Review the vision you imagined a few exercises ago and decide if it's something that can be created in one go or if it will take a series of steps. If it's one step, write that down. If it's many, write those down, too, leaving enough space between each to drill down into smaller and smaller steps until you arrive at one, clear action.

As you review these steps and substeps, consider the order of things. What can you do right now? What must wait until later? And so on.

Similar to the last exercise, determine when you will do the first step and give yourself a deadline. If you feel comfortable with this, also consider telling a trusted friend or mentor about your plans for accountability.

After you complete each action, take a moment to reflect on how it feels to accomplish it. Think about how much closer you are now to your next cycle. Let that emotion sink in and fill you up with joy as you work through your next set of actions.

RECOGNIZING THE ADJACENT POSSIBLE

Where we end up isn't always where we intended to go, but it's often just as sweet or even better than we could've imagined.

There may be moments in your bending journey when life throws you a curveball. You may have had a very clear vision and action plan for fulfilling that vision. You may have felt all the right feelings and thought all the right thoughts and for whatever reason, the harder you pushed to create a specific cycle, absolutely nothing was turning out how you wanted.

You are at a crossroads. You could stay the course until you either get the cycle you envisioned, regardless of every setback/setup. Or, you could pause, reflect, and look for the adjacent possible that may have opened up.

- Are you suddenly being told that while you're great with *A*, people think you'd be even better with *B*?

- Have you received a call out of the blue for an opportunity you never thought about but that intrigues and inspires you?

- Have you started living parts of your desired cycle but realized it's not actually what you wanted?

In all of these scenarios, look for the adjacent possible. Where might these external catalysts be pointing you toward that you hadn't considered before? How are you going to respond?

The vision sets the course. The imagination and emotion fuel the journey. But the real excitement comes from the unexpected adventures along the way. If you take a step off the intended path for something new, what could you be opening up in your life?

THE BENDSTYLE PROFILE
(Life Edition)

he final chapter of this book, Chapter 9: Pay It Forward, highlighted the natural next step for any bender. When you bend long enough, it's impossible to *not* positively influence those around you, even if you do it by accident. If you're curious about how you might already be impacting those around you, the **BendStyle Profile** will identify how you naturally bend reality in your own sphere of influence. It measures your default "blend" across three roles—**Architect of Possibility** (how you create space for new ideas), **Catalyst of Growth** (how you work with emotion, trust, and courage), and **Steward of Outcomes** (how you turn intention into results)—along with a quick check of how well you're leading the **Reality Cycle** itself.

Don't overthink your answers. Score each statement **1 / 3 / 5 (1 = Rarely true | 3 = Sometimes true | 5 = Consistently true)** based on what's *most true of you lately*, not who you wish you were on your best day.

Then rank your three role totals from strongest to weakest to find your BendStyle Type, and use the coaching prompt that follows to apply what you learned in the next seven days. Awareness is helpful, but application is where reality actually starts to bend.

PART 1: THE ASSESSMENT

Architect of Possibility (Safety + Reframing + Experimentation)

1. I create space for bold ideas without immediately judging whether they'll work.

2. People in my world feel safe telling the truth, disagreeing, or challenging "how we've always done it."

3. I treat mistakes as learning—and I help others do the same.

4. When we're stuck, I naturally look for a different angle or a better story we could live from.

5. I make time for exploration—trying small new approaches instead of repeating the same patterns.

6. I shape conversations so they create imagination, not just updates or venting.

7. I help others take ownership instead of waiting to be told what to do.

8. I protect space for what matters (growth, creativity, healing, connection) from the tyranny of urgent stuff.

9. I ask, "What might we be missing?" before I assume the options are limited.

10. I tend to see constraints as creative boundaries, not permanent walls.

11. I invite others to bring ideas—even if they're rough, weird, or unfinished.

12. I help people turn complaints into constructive possibilities ("If that's not working, what do we want instead?").

ARCHITECT SUBTOTAL: ☐ / 60

Catalyst of Growth (Emotion + Trust + Courage)

1. I can sense the emotional "weather" in a room and name it when it matters.

2. I'm willing to be real and vulnerable in a way that builds trust, not drama.

3. I help people separate what they feel from what they assume—then turn emotion into wise action.

4. In hard conversations, I aim for both truth and connection—not one at the expense of the other.

5. I ask questions like: "What are you feeling—and what do you need right now?"

6. I notice effort and growth, not just results, and I say it out loud.

7. When things go sideways, I help people interpret the moment in a way that builds courage.

8. People tend to open up to me early—before small problems become big ones.

9. I can stay calm around strong emotions without shutting down or snapping back.

10. I help people name what they really care about underneath the surface argument.

11. I'M QUICK TO REPAIR RUPTURES (MISUNDERSTANDINGS, TENSION, HURT) INSTEAD OF LETTING THEM LINGER.

12. I CAN CHALLENGE SOMEONE WITH HONESTY IN A WAY THAT STILL LEAVES THEM FEELING SEEN.

CATALYST SUBTOTAL: ☐ / 60

Steward of Outcomes (Follow-through + Ownership + Results)

1. I TURN GOOD INTENTIONS INTO SIMPLE PLANS WITH CLEAR NEXT STEPS AND OWNERSHIP.

2. I MAKE COMMITMENTS CLEAR—AND I FOLLOW UP IN A WAY THAT SUPPORTS PROGRESS WITHOUT CONTROLLING PEOPLE.

3. PEOPLE AROUND ME KNOW WHAT "SUCCESS" LOOKS LIKE BECAUSE WE NAME IT PLAINLY.

4. I TREAT RESULTS AS FEEDBACK, NOT A FINAL VERDICT ON ANYONE'S WORTH OR ABILITY.

5. I CAN BALANCE HOPE WITH REALITY (TIME, ENERGY, MONEY, CONSTRAINTS, CAPACITY).

6. I CELEBRATE PROGRESS WHILE STILL HOLDING A HEALTHY STANDARD.

7. I USE SIMPLE SCOREBOARDS—PROOF, SIGNALS, OR VISIBLE RESULTS—TO KEEP US HONEST AND MOVING.

8. AFTER SOMETHING HAPPENS (GOOD OR BAD), I HELP TURN IT INTO A LESSON THAT IMPROVES WHAT WE DO NEXT.

9. I TEND TO FINISH WHAT WE START—EVEN WHEN THE EXCITEMENT WEARS OFF.

10. I'M WILLING TO MAKE THE HARD CALL (SIMPLIFY, CUT, RESCHEDULE, SAY NO) TO PROTECT WHAT MATTERS MOST.

11. I CAN TURN BIG GOALS INTO SMALL "NEXT RIGHT STEPS" THAT FEEL DOABLE TODAY.

12. I DON'T JUST TALK ABOUT CHANGE—I BUILD RHYTHMS THAT MAKE CHANGE SUSTAINABLE (HABITS, CHECK-INS, ROUTINES).

STEWARD SUBTOTAL: ☐ / 60

Reality Cycle Check – 10 items

1. I CAN IDENTIFY THE STORY/PERCEPTION DRIVING WHAT'S HAPPENING RIGHT NOW.

2. I CAN NAME THE EMOTION UNDERNEATH RESISTANCE, PROCRASTINATION, CONFLICT, OR DISCOURAGEMENT.

3. I HELP PEOPLE IMAGINE A BETTER FUTURE WITH SPECIFIC DETAIL—NOT VAGUE HOPE.

4. I CAN CHALLENGE LIMITING BELIEFS (MINE OR OTHERS') WITHOUT SHAMING OR OVERPOWERING.

5. I PREFER SMALL EXPERIMENTS OVER ALL-OR-NOTHING PROMISES.

6. I PAY ATTENTION TO OUTCOMES AND LET THEM RESHAPE THE STORY WE TELL GOING FORWARD.

7. I CAN WORK FUTURE-BACK: OUTCOME → ACTION → BELIEFS → IMAGINATION → EMOTION → PERCEPTION.

8. I can coach someone through the cycle without taking over or rescuing them.

9. I notice when "setting a goal" is replacing the deeper work of buy-in, belief, and emotional fuel.

10. I help people reinterpret outcomes so they stay engaged instead of quitting.

REALITY CYCLE TOTAL: ☐ / 50

Score	Reality Cycle
40-50	You lead the cycle consistently
30-39	Strong foundation; you drift under pressure
20-29	Often stuck in old loops
10-19	You're likely leading outcomes without tending the inner levers

PART 2: INTERPRETING THE RESULTS

Role Totals

ARCHITECT OF POSSIBILITY: ☐ / 60

CATALYST OF GROWTH: ☐ / 60

STEWARD OF OUTCOMES: ☐ / 60

Using the scores from your role totals, rank your three role subtotals:

FIRST (HIGHEST): _______________________________________

SECOND: _______________________________________

THIRD (LOWEST): _______________________________________

- Your **highest** role is your *Nature Zone*—you do it naturally, especially under pressure.

- Your **middle** role is your *Flex Zone*—it shows up when you're intentional.

- Your **lowest** role is your *Growth Edge*—not because you're broken, but because it costs you more.

Your Nature Zone is where you're going to perform at the highest. It's where you have the most capacity to continue to bend and continue to grow. It may sound simple and easy to lean into what you already do well, but most people tend to value these natural parts of themselves the least. And they certainly value it less than those who are benefiting from it. Here's the lens reframe: These natural talents are actually the most important when you consider the fact that *this is where people are benefitting from you the most*. This is where they're getting the most value from you. That's a big deal! So why wouldn't you focus on magnifying that? Why wouldn't you want to build on that impact?

As you lean into your Nature Zone, I want you to also consider your Growth Edge. We're all good at certain things, but we're also really not great at others. That's okay. But ask yourself *why?* Why do I struggle with creating space for new ideas, or working with emotion, trust, and courage, or turning intention into results? What are the dynamics at play here? Is it because what's required here is just so far from your natural hardwiring? Or is it that you haven't been intentional in strengthening these skills?

This ranking also creates your specific blend order from highest Leadership Role to lowest and identifies your BendStyle Type. (For more information on each type, go to Appendix E: The Six BendStyle Types (all-in-one profiles).

**ARCHITECT → CATALYST → STEWARD
= THE VISION IGNITER**

**ARCHITECT → STEWARD → CATALYST
= THE BUILDER-DESIGNER**

**CATALYST → ARCHITECT → STEWARD
= THE HEARTFELT INNOVATOR**

**CATALYST → STEWARD → ARCHITECT
= THE CHANGE COACH**

**STEWARD → ARCHITECT → CATALYST
= THE MOMENTUM MAKER**

**STEWARD → CATALYST → ARCHITECT
= THE ACCOUNTABLE ENCOURAGER**

YOUR BENDSTYLE TYPE:

____

BENDING IN BUSINESS

ruly, everyone is a leader in their own sphere of influence regardless of title, position, or level of authority. But with my business roots, I couldn't miss the chance to connect Reality Bending to traditional leadership. If you've read either of my other two books, you've probably picked up on some similar themes.

Many of the professionals and celebrities I mention in *Be Weird: How to Succeed in Life and Business Simply by Being You* and *The 4 Dimensions of Culture: And the Leaders Who Shape Them* are Reality Benders—it's how they became who they are. I just honestly hadn't realized it at the time, and coined the term Reality Benders only when I started writing this book. So consider this the chapter that brings all those past stories together.

Entrepreneurs and leaders naturally lend themselves to Reality Bending. Entrepreneurial leaders are naturally curious visionary risk-takers who do whatever it takes to bring a business to life. They begin with an idea and over time, create something extraordinary—often out of nothing—that either improves upon the past or brings into reality things that hadn't been imagined ever before. These include Steve Jobs and Apple, Blake Mycoskie and TOMS, Walt Disney and Walt Disney Studio, Ed Catmull and Pixar. The list goes on and on.

This isn't to say that Bender leaders aren't without their faults. No Reality Bender is perfect, but the point is that they grow from mistakes and bad takes and continue to help those in their spheres of influence bend reality as well.

In the world of Benders, leaders are architects and catalysts. They are the creators of cultures where people discover better versions of themselves. Their most significant contribution is guiding others into cycles of growth, self-mastery, and new possibilities. The core question for the Bender leader is not "What must be done?" but "How will I, as a Reality-Bending leader, help others bend their reality toward growth, confidence, and new possibilities?"

In my life-long personal study of leadership, there appear to be three main characteristics of great leaders. They are Architects of Possibility, Catalysts of Growth, and Stewards of Outcomes. And again, even though they do develop all three characteristics over time, Bender leaders use these characteristics as situations require.

The Architect of Possibility: *They design cultures that invite experimentation and reframing, and create safe spaces for bold ideas and rapid learning.*

Bill Gore, of W. L. Gore & Associates, Inc., built this type of Reality Bending into the fabric (no pun intended) of the GORE-TEX company. After leaving DuPont in 1958 to cofound his own company with his wife, Gore created what he called a lattice organizational structure[23] that essentially empowers every person to be a leader. There are no bosses, only leaders. There are no titles; everyone is called an "associate." Associates have to agree to follow said leaders, otherwise they're no longer leaders. But more incredibly, the four principles guiding everyday operations create an environment that encourages every associate to take ownership and develop the kind of innovative ideas that have shaped GORE-TEX products for over fifty years:[24]

> **FREEDOM:** Associates are free to encourage each other to grow and learn.

- **FAIRNESS:** Everyone should act with fairness towards each other.
- **COMMITMENT:** Associates make their own commitments they are expected to keep.
- **WATERLINE:** Any action that impacts other parts of the company or the company as a whole must first be run through a committee.

The idea is that if GORE-TEX is a boat, there are potentially good risks or actions (impacts hitting above the waterline that can rock the boat but not sink it) and there are bad risks or actions (impacts hitting below the waterline that sink the boat).

Along with these core principles, GORE-TEX has "dabble" time—portions of the day or week set aside for everyone to experiment with new products or ideas.[25]

In establishing an unconventional business structure, Gore created the kind of workplace that rewards imagination and follow-through and taps into the emotional buy-in of literally every employee—leading to the kind of imagination, emotion, and possibility thinking that bends reality.

The Catalyst of Growth: *They cultivate emotional intelligence and vulnerability as leadership tools and model how to name and channel emotions into constructive action.*

While studying industrial design in college, a certain professor challenged students to solve a social issue through design. So Veronika Scott rose to that challenge. She had a vision for what *could* be and that, like most new realities, was rooted in imagination. She created a coat that could be used as a sleeping bag or an over-the-shoulder bag for people experiencing homelessness in her local Detroit community.[26] But as she worked with a small group of homeless folks to perfect the design for everyday use, one woman told her that she needed a job more than she needed a coat. (A perfect example of an adjacent possibility that wasn't even on Veronika's radar at the time.)

Understanding that she could create a bigger impact, Veronika founded the nonprofit organization Empowerment Plan, which employs homeless parents to manufacture the coats and break their own reality cycle of homelessness. Today, the organization has become a workforce development organization that supports its community with more than just employment and coats, but also through childcare, education, and transportation.

Veronika looked directly at the need in front of her, something most of us shy away from, and used the talents and tools at her disposal to create real change for the people within her sphere of influence. She is a Catalyst of Growth.

The Steward of Outcomes: *They balance ambition with execution and clear accountability, translating vision into measurable experiments and results.*

William Kamkwamba's story is now well-documented in the 2009 memoir and 2019 Netflix movie of the same name, *The Boy Who Harnessed the Wind*, but as it goes, he was around fourteen years old when he started experimenting with wind energy.[27, 28] Growing up in a rural village in Malawi, he had to leave school when a drought ruined his family's finances.

However, this setback set William up for something much greater. His natural curiosity led him to the library to read school textbooks, where he first saw a picture of a windmill and learned how it worked. He then started collecting cast-off pieces and parts from bicycles, cars, anything he could find and use to build a small windmill for his family's home. Hooking it up to a car battery, he was able to store the electrical energy created throughout the day to power a lightbulb and small appliances. Soon after, he started building more windmills and a solar-powered water pump for the village. But this was just the beginning.

Eventually, William attended Dartmouth, where he majored in environmental studies and took classes in engineering, while also co-founding a nonprofit called The Moving Windmills Project. To this day, he continues to improve life for those in poverty-stricken communities.

While he may not have started with a specific vision in mind, William knew that he could lift up his family and village through ingenuity, innovation, and a lot of experimentation. He didn't just cast vision for a new reality and walk away; he became a Steward of Outcomes, with deep emotional ties to the reality he was creating.

———————

Sometimes leaders found companies, and sometimes they receive the title when they're born— but more commonly, and more impactfully, leaders rise to meet the problems of their time. When this happens, they're not just responding to a need; they're bending reality for themselves and those around them. They're helping the people within their spheres of influence escape from the comfort of their current cycles to be more. If we view leadership through the lens of the Bender Leader, every team meeting, every hard conversation, every challenge becomes an opportunity for new possibilities. They become the transformative catalyst, the agent of change for others. They ask the question: "How will I help those in my sphere bend their reality?"

Bender Leaders use the cycle as both a map and a mirror. They guide teams through cycles of growth and learning, and they reflect on outcomes to define the future. They invite the team to co-create the vision of the future. This buy-in also engages, excites, and unites everyone to work for this common cause.

With a picture of a new reality set, the Bender Leader encourages the experimentation that leads to innovation and continuous improvement necessary to realize that new future. So while the individual often works the cycle like this:

PERCEPTION → EMOTION → IMAGINATION → BELIEFS → ACTION → OUTCOME

the Leader starts with the end in mind:

OUTCOME → ACTION → BELIEFS → IMAGINATION → EMOTION → PERCEPTION

Don't skip past this reordering too quickly. Good leaders need to understand where they are leading their teams (outcome) and work backwards to change the viewpoint (perception) of their team members, who likely can't even imagine getting there. Leaders train themselves to see this whole picture—Outcome → Action → Beliefs → Imagination → Emotion → Perception—and bring it to life in a way their team can understand and rally behind.

I started exploring the cultural side of Reality Bending in *The 4 Dimensions of Culture*—the idea that culture is the most important aspect of a business, and that the organization becomes a shadow of the leader. The reason this is true is *because* of the Reality Cycle. A leader who leads the cycle naturally creates an environment that brings out the best in everyone, and that allows everyone to improve their own cycles.

WHY CONVENTIONAL LEADERSHIP MISSES THE POINT

That's easy enough, Greg. I can hear you thinking it. Most leaders I've worked with can create a vision, present it to the team, and even get some buy-in and enthusiasm for the plan from the top, but in ninety days, everyone will abandon the new plan for the old one for all the same reasons people stop going to the gym: They're not *seeing* the results they expect; it's too hard to keep going without a guarantee that what you're doing will work; etc.

The leader has fallen into the trap of thinking that goal-setting in and of itself is inspirational.

We all do at some point.

I've led countless strategy sessions over the years, and what I've learned is that they always fall flat. Leaders will make plans based on their desired outcomes and then tell their teams, "Here are our goals. Here's what you're accountable for. Here's how I'm going to do my one-on-ones each month to see how you're progressing..." But the problem is that these goals are outcome-focused; it's Business School 101. Yet this conventional approach forgets the *emotional* side of Bob and Bernadette in their windowless cubicles. They aren't nearly as excited about *your* vision, yet they are the ones who will have to execute the necessary changes to achieve the desired outcomes. Everything the leaders take back to their teams are scoreboards and KPIs.

That's why strategy sessions fail. It is a vision for a new reality without understanding the intermediate steps—Action → Beliefs → Imagination → Emotion—that connect vision to outcome.

Most leaders forget that people are not inspired by goals alone. Most leaders forget about the emotional side of the humans on their teams. They forget that mindsets must change for behaviors to change, and both must change to get different outcomes.

Bender Leaders know they first must work on the hearts and minds of the individuals they've been entrusted to lead. This is how they motivate and inspire. Then they can focus on the outcomes. (Even as I write this, I worry that some of you are rolling your eyes at me and saying, "All right Greg, enough with the touchy-feely stuff." Here's the deal, though. If you ignore this piece of the equation, you may get your team to show up for their shift, but you won't have their buy-in for the new reality you hope to build. I've coached enough leaders who have tried it both ways, and I promise you, the *heart* element is critical to bending reality.)

Be aware of this fact.

As a leader, you are always making people feel something. Those feelings and emotions are the fuel for strong commitment and sustainable effort. Smart leaders don't try to take emotion out of the workplace; they cultivate emotions and build emotional attachment to the desired goals and outcomes.

Here's an example of how this might play out.

A manager is in a performance meeting with someone on the team who fell short of the prescribed goals. A regular leader says, "So, the goal this quarter was a 5 percent increase in sales, but you only achieved 2 percent. Because you fell short, we'll have to create a Performance Improvement Plan for the next quarter. If you can't meet those goals, we have to have another meeting..."

The Bender Leader says, "The goal this quarter was a 5 percent increase in sales, but you only achieved a 2 percent increase. We'll have to create a Performance Improvement Plan, but man, every time I saw you in action, your work ethic was unbelievable. Look how much you've grown since joining the company two years ago! Let's talk about what worked for you and how I can help..."

If people can imagine it, they can achieve it. That's Reality-Bending leadership.

The Bender Leader doesn't gloss over less-than-ideal outcomes. Instead, they help their team reinterpret those outcomes so they're inspired instead of discouraged (changing their perception.) They're always finding a way to keep people emotionally engaged (engaging their emotions.) They become the external catalyst for others to help them engage their imaginations. If people can imagine it, they can achieve it. That's Reality-Bending leadership.

THE LEADERSHIP MINDSET SHIFT

Bender Leaders want to be more than just a great CEO or a great VP. They want to be Architects of Possibility, Catalysts for Growth, and Stewards of Outcomes for those they lead. And they do this when they quit leading *people* and start leading the *cycle*. (Go read that again and let it sink in.)

Imagine a man who wants to create the adventure of a lifetime for his family. He spends a few weeks coming up with a plan and decides that the best thing to do is rent out their house and travel around the country in an RV. So he gathers everyone into the living room one night to put on the presentation of a lifetime. He says, "Family, I think we need to travel around the country in an RV for a year. We'll go to…" and as he names the national parks and historic monuments they'll visit, he shows pictures to really put his vision in their minds.

"Of course this means we'll need to sell some stuff," he says. "Get rid of the second car, rent a storage unit for certain things, and maybe let the dog stay with Grandma and Grandpa while we're gone."

You can imagine the upheaval. The youngest immediately bursts out crying at the thought of leaving Fido behind. The middle child, who's going to start high school in the fall, is beside herself. She'll never find her place in the hierarchy if she leaves now. And the oldest couldn't possibly live without his gaming systems. You can only imagine what's going through the wife's mind. (I'd write it here, but I'm trying to keep this book suitable for all audiences.)

That's a picture of traditional leadership—*you* create a vision and try to get your team onboard. But even if they're not, you follow the numbers because that's how you'll survive. That's leading *people*, for good or bad.

There's a better way. A more powerful way. This is leading the *cycle*:

"Family, how would you like to travel the country, making memories, 'skipping' school for a year, and doing all those things we talked about when we were younger—I'm looking at you, Donna…"

Instead of creating a pre-planned itinerary, everyone has a chance to decide where the family goes. Instead of telling everyone they have to get rid of their stuff, you run the numbers together and understand that the best way to afford this trip is by renting the house, and the natural consequence of living in such tight quarters is that you can't take everything with you. Instead of pushing a vision top-down, you create the environment that allows everyone to feel inspired and valuable, and to experiment with innovation (the oldest is going to look into a solar-powered generator to run his favorite tech). You cast the vision together. You engage the collective emotions of all. You jumpstart the mindset needed to eventually bring out the desired outcome (priceless memories).

This is the power of the Leader.

No matter how big or small your team or company, it is entirely possible to lead the cycle, which results in more powerful outcomes than just achieving a 6 percent increase in sales. When you lead the cycle, you cast the vision—like what you would like to see in a year, five years, ten years? But then you invite your team into imagining the details and the process of how to get there. You work future-back.

This works even, and especially, in times of crisis. If you're leading people toward a vision, you must start with their mindset and belief systems. If they believe they can create the collective vision, if they are emotionally invested in that collective vision, they will have the fortitude to weather the storms. For the times when they need a lift, that's where you, the Bender Leader, help reframe the outcomes to mentally and emotionally set them up to work with whatever happens next—you help them engage with infinite possibilities.

Rewrite the narrative. Change the lens. Create a new cycle.

LEADING THE CYCLE IN ACTION

Believe me when I say I understand how challenging and rewarding it can be to lead a team and a business. That's part of what's kept me going for so long. I also know that implementing any kind of change carries a certain amount of risk. But when you lead the cycle instead of people, you're not only creating a better culture in the office, you're also giving the individuals in your care the tools they need to bend life beyond the cubicle. That's the challenge. That's the call.

You don't need to be in the C-suite to lead the cycle. However big or small your team, invite them into the bending process at every part of the cycle. Make the culture safe for people to imagine and dream, to be emotional and vulnerable, to test out ideas and overcome limitations. As your collective performance skyrockets, others will notice the positive changes, so don't be surprised if they ask about what you're doing. And this is a good thing—just imagine how far you can go with a company full of Master Benders!

To make sure this chapter includes clear steps and strategies that you can try out today, I created a Leading the Cycle Step-by-Step guide. Beginning with imagination, emotion, and perception, and finishing up with actions and outcomes, I explain how each concept shows up in a business environment and provide a suggested activity to test out with your team. These aren't the only ways to bring the Reality Cycle concepts into the office, but they can give you a place to start.

However, I want you to make leading the cycle your own. If something doesn't work for you, or if you come up with new and engaging ways to bend with a team, by all means use them! But for now, consider these exercises plug-and-play ready. (The examples below are from actual people I've worked with; I've just changed the names to keep them anonymous.)

STEP 1. IMAGINATION
Building Worlds of Possibility

In a Bender business culture, imagination is a strategy for building worlds of possibility with discipline. Imagination, when harnessed, becomes a strategic engine. Leaders guide teams through "futurecasting," scenario planning, and collaborative ideation that expands the range of feasible futures and aligns actions toward achieving desired realities. "Futurecasting" is a form of future-back thinking used to facilitate structured sessions where team members sketch a future that has "already occurred." Then working backward, they answer these questions:

- What thinking was required to achieve this outcome?
- What mindset produced this outcome?
- What perception allowed us to believe it was possible?
- What does it feel like to experience this outcome?

In doing this, Bender Leaders create a safe environment for bold, innovative ideas. And the twist? Treat instances of unsuccessful tests as valuable (think like Edison) and recognize learning as a fundamental to innovation and creativity.

When Alex, the CTO of a startup and one of my coaching clients, faced brutal competition, he hosted a "futurecasting" session. He brought his small team into a conference room and had them close their eyes, while verbally sketching the company's future as if it had already happened. He wrote down their ideas on a whiteboard, and as they finished the exercise, they decided which ideas they wanted to try and how and when to execute them.

Through this exercise, the team came up with some wild innovations, new revenue streams, and a breakthrough product idea that arrived not from planning but from collaboration and collective imagination. The team became creators of possibility, bending forward to what could be.

Encourage teams to share stories of when a new idea (even a tiny one) bent reality for the better. "What happened the last time we imagined something bold and acted on it?"

STEP 2. EMOTION
Cultivating the Emotional Climate

Emotion is not noise to be managed away; it is the fuel that powers perception and the curiosity to imagine different futures. In Chapter 5, we learned that cultivating authentic emotional energy is the linchpin of transformation. To emotionally engage their teams, Bender Leaders cultivate an authentic emotional culture that encourages vulnerability, trust, and constructive risk-taking.

One approach is through Emotion Mapping and Energy Check-Ins, especially during periods of transition or the end of a quarter or project. When the team comes together, start meetings by naming and acknowledging the dominant emotion in the room, then guide a brief reflection on how that emotion affects decision-making. This practice acknowledges and normalizes emotion and creates a common language for adjustment. In this way, the Bender Leader teaches team members to distinguish emotion from judgment, then convert emotional data into actionable steps (e.g., "We're anxious about this risk; let's design a safe experiment to reduce uncertainty.")

A note on Emotion Mapping and Energy Check-Ins. This can sometimes be difficult to do with large team meetings, especially in mixed hierarchy environments where people may be hesitant to speak up. If you notice this, consider doing individual check-ins or even send out an energy survey to get the conversation going.

In one team brainstorming meeting, a manager noticed her team's growing fear about a merger. Rather than mask it, she led an "Emotion Mapping" exercise: Each person named and mapped their strongest emotion on the board. As vulnerability surfaced, the room became charged not with fear, but with connection. People saw they weren't alone, and anxiety gave way to collective resolve. Imagination was freed by the courage of naming emotion.

Reality Bender Practice–Energy Check-In

Begin every team session by checking the emotional weather. "What energy is present here? How do we want to feel to create the best outcome?"

STEP 3. PERCEPTION
Breaking the Spell of Limitation

Leadership expands when you notice and reframe collective narratives by challenging the stories people tell about themselves, about work, and about what's possible. When a team confronts an obstacle, deadline pressure, resource constraints, or conflicting priorities, the leader questions the automatic story and probes for truth beneath the noise. By asking targeted questions, the leader disrupts the limiting thinking and provides a lens, new thinking, and cultivated emotions, leading to desired outcomes.

Consider reality-reframing sessions at the start of significant initiatives. Begin these meetings with simple questions: "What story are we buying into? What would be true if we rewrote the narrative? What's one new story we can test this week?" Encourage team members to discuss both the current state and a preferred future state. Then model the cognitive shift from the old narrative to the new one.

One Monday morning, a project team was mired in complaints about an impossible deadline. The Reality Bender leader didn't dispute the facts—instead, she paused the narrative. She asked:

- "What's the story we're buying into? What's TRUE and what's just noise?"

- "If you could rewrite this story, what would you say instead?"

The spell broke. Perspective shifted. "We're smart. We've done impossible things before." The team moved from victimhood to possibility.

Reality Bender Practice – Reality Reframing

Before making decisions, stop and ask: "Which reality am I operating from—old stories, or new potential?"

STEP 4. ACTION
The Move from Vision to Reality

Imagination without action is fantasy. So Reality Bender Leaders know how to champion commitment from their team—the kind of commitment that turns ideas into outcomes. Action is the engine that transforms imagination into reality. Bender Leaders translate bold ideas into concrete experiments, accountable ownership, and measurable progress.

Like GORE-TEX, consider the commitment contract approach: For every bold idea, specify one experiment, an owner, a timeline, and a success metric. Make sure clear KPIs are established and communicated. Treat experiments as learning opportunities rather than final judgments. The point here is to emphasize accountability and ownership through regular check-ins that focus on learning milestones rather than just outputs.

In a manufacturing firm, a supervisor launched "Commitment Contracts." For every new innovative idea, the team wrote down one experimental action and who was accountable for it.

Progress accelerated. What could have been wishful thinking became prototypes, then pilots, then winning outcomes.

Reality Bender Practice – Bend the Cycle Workshop

Regularly hold team meetings and reflect on one cycle (what was the initial perception, emotion, imagination, action, and outcome?) Ask: "How did we bend reality—and what's the next level?"

STEP 5. OUTCOME
The Ripple Effect and the Next Cycle

Outcomes should serve not as final destinations but as catalysts for future cycles. Every outcome becomes the beginning of a new cycle. Each result, whether it is a completed project, an improved process, or a transformation in team culture, creates new opportunities, encouraging renewed perspectives, engagement, and innovation. In a Reality-Bending culture, failure is feedback and success is a step forward, not a resting place. Teams celebrate both, knowing that every cycle changes who they are and moves them closer to the best version of themselves.

After major milestones, host a Reality Rewrite and Celebration session to extract lessons, reset and reframe the narrative based on new learnings, and set the stage for the next cycle. Emphasize continuous improvement. Recognize progress openly, analyze missteps transparently, and reiterate the value of iteration.

After a product launch sputtered, the team held a "Reality Rewrite": Each member shared what they learned and how the outcome bent their thinking for next time. The next launch was a record-breaker.

Reality Bender Practice–Celebration and Reset

After milestones, pause to ask: "What did we bend? How are we different? What reality will we cultivate next?"

Leadership is a daily practice. It's courageously reframing reality, cultivating and harnessing emotions, investing in imagination, driving a strong commitment to action, and celebrating every outcome as the beginning of the next evolution. The Reality Cycle is more than just a tool. It's a framework for building a high performance culture and a work environment that stimulates innovative thought and team collaboration.

You were meant to become a conduit—someone through whom clarity, imagination, and belief flow outward into the lives of others. That is significance.

Yet significance alone is not the end of the journey.

Because once you help others bend their reality, something even bigger begins to take shape. What started as an individual decision to see differently begins to influence how groups think, how teams act, and how future leaders lead.

This is where Reality Bending moves beyond moments and into systems.

Beyond influence and into continuity.

Beyond significance and into legacy.

It's about how leaders build an organizational culture that protects imagination. Where beliefs are built intentionally. Where people don't just succeed, but grow, contribute, and multiply impact long after you've moved on. This is what all business leaders should aspire to.

THE BENDSTYLE PROFILE
(Business Edition)

fter reading about bending in business, you may already know what kind of a Bender Leader you are. However, if you're not sure or if you'd like confirmation, I created the **BendStyle Profile Business Edition)** based upon the Life Edition in Appendix B. Just like the Life Edition assessment, this BendStyle Profile will identify how you naturally bend reality in your own sphere of influence at work.

If you've already taken the Life Edition, you can skip ahead to Part 1: The Assessment.

If you haven't, just know that this profile measures your default "blend" across three roles—**Architect of Possibility** (how you create space for new ideas), **Catalyst of Growth** (how you work with emotion, trust, and courage), and **Steward of Outcomes** (how you turn intention into results)—along with a quick check of how well you're leading the **Reality Cycle** itself.

Don't overthink your answers. Score each statement **1 / 3 / 5 (1 = Rarely true | 3 = Sometimes true | 5 = Consistently true)** based on what's *most true of you lately*, not who you wish you were on your best day.

Then rank your three role totals from strongest to weakest to find your BendStyle Type, and use the coaching prompt that follows to apply what you learned in the next seven days. Awareness is helpful, but application is where reality actually starts to bend.

PART 1: THE ASSESSMENT

Architect of Possibility (Culture + Safety + Experimentation)

1. I CREATE SPACE FOR BOLD IDEAS WITHOUT IMMEDIATELY JUDGING FEASIBILITY.

2. MY TEAM FEELS SAFE CHALLENGING "HOW WE'VE ALWAYS DONE IT."

3. I REWARD LEARNING EVEN WHEN AN EXPERIMENT DOESN'T WORK.

4. I REGULARLY INVITE PEOPLE TO REFRAME PROBLEMS INTO POSSIBILITIES.

5. I MAKE TIME FOR EXPLORATION (DABBLE/SANDBOX/PILOTS).

6. I DESIGN MEETINGS THAT PRODUCE IMAGINATION, NOT JUST UPDATES.

7. I ENCOURAGE OWNERSHIP—PEOPLE LEAD WITHOUT NEEDING PERMISSION.

8. I PROTECT CREATIVE WORK FROM URGENCY AND CONSTANT FIREFIGHTING.

9. BEFORE CHOOSING A PLAN, I ASK: "WHAT OPTIONS ARE WE NOT SEEING YET?"

10. I TREAT CONSTRAINTS (TIME, BUDGET, RESOURCES) AS CREATIVE BOUNDARIES, NOT DEAD ENDS.

11. I INVITE ROUGH DRAFTS AND IMPERFECT IDEAS EARLY, SO INNOVATION HAS ROOM TO GROW.

12. I HELP TEAMS CONVERT COMPLAINTS INTO CONSTRUCTIVE POSSIBILITIES ("IF THAT'S NOT WORKING, WHAT WOULD?").

ARCHITECT SUBTOTAL: ☐ / 60

Catalyst of Growth (Emotion + Trust + Vulnerability)

1. I NOTICE THE EMOTIONAL "WEATHER" AND NAME IT WHEN NEEDED.

2. I MODEL VULNERABILITY WITHOUT LOSING LEADERSHIP STRENGTH.

3. I HELP PEOPLE SEPARATE EMOTION FROM JUDGMENT AND TURN IT INTO ACTION.

4. IN HARD CONVERSATIONS, I AIM FOR CONNECTION + CLARITY, NOT JUST CORRECTION.

5. I ASK: "WHAT ARE YOU FEELING—AND WHAT DO YOU NEED TO MOVE FORWARD?"

6. I VALIDATE EFFORT AND GROWTH EVEN WHEN RESULTS FALL SHORT.

7. I HELP PEOPLE INTERPRET SETBACKS IN WAYS THAT BUILD CONFIDENCE.

8. I CULTIVATE TRUST SO PEOPLE TELL THE TRUTH EARLY, NOT LATE.

9. I CAN STAY STEADY WHEN EMOTIONS RUN HIGH (CONFLICT, FEAR, UNCERTAINTY) WITHOUT SHUTTING DOWN.

10. I HELP PEOPLE NAME WHAT THEY TRULY CARE ABOUT UNDERNEATH THE SURFACE ARGUMENT.

11. I REPAIR TENSION QUICKLY (MISUNDERSTANDINGS, FRICTION, UNMET EXPECTATIONS) INSTEAD OF LETTING IT LINGER.

12. I CAN CHALLENGE SOMEONE WITH HONESTY IN A WAY THAT STILL LEAVES THEM FEELING SEEN AND CAPABLE.

CATALYST SUBTOTAL: ☐ / 60

Steward of Outcomes (Execution + Ownership + Results)

1. I TRANSLATE VISION INTO EXPERIMENTS WITH OWNERS, TIMELINES, AND METRICS.

2. I MAKE COMMITMENTS CLEAR—AND I FOLLOW UP WITHOUT MICROMANAGING.

3. MY TEAM KNOWS WHAT "WINNING" LOOKS LIKE IN MEASURABLE TERMS.

4. I TREAT OUTCOMES AS FEEDBACK FOR THE NEXT CYCLE, NOT THE END.

5. I BALANCE AMBITION WITH REALITY (RESOURCES, CONSTRAINTS, SEQUENCING).

6. I CELEBRATE PROGRESS AND ALSO INSIST ON ACCOUNTABILITY.

7. I BUILD SIMPLE SCOREBOARDS THAT HELP LEARNING—NOT JUST PRESSURE.

8. I DEBRIEF IN WAYS THAT CONVERT LESSONS INTO BETTER NEXT ACTIONS.

9. I TEND TO FINISH WHAT WE START—EVEN AFTER THE INITIAL EXCITEMENT WEARS OFF.

10. I'M WILLING TO MAKE THE HARD CALL (SIMPLIFY, CUT SCOPE, SAY NO, RESEQUENCE) TO PROTECT THE GOAL.

11. I CAN TURN BIG GOALS INTO SMALL "NEXT RIGHT STEPS" THAT FEEL DOABLE THIS WEEK.

12. I BUILD RHYTHMS THAT MAKE EXECUTION SUSTAINABLE (CADENCE, CHECK-INS, REVIEW CYCLES), NOT DEPENDENT ON WILLPOWER.

STEWARD SUBTOTAL: ☐ / 60

Reality Cycle Check (Business)

1. I CAN IDENTIFY THE STORY/PERCEPTION DRIVING OUR CURRENT SITUATION.

2. I CAN NAME THE EMOTION UNDERNEATH RESISTANCE OR DISENGAGEMENT.

3. I HELP PEOPLE IMAGINE A BETTER FUTURE IN SPECIFIC DETAIL.

4. I CHALLENGE LIMITING BELIEFS WITHOUT SHAMING.

5. I TURN IDEAS INTO SMALL EXPERIMENTS RATHER THAN ALL-OR-NOTHING PLANS.

6. I TRACK OUTCOMES AND USE THEM TO RESET THE NARRATIVE.

7. I CAN WORK FUTURE-BACK: OUTCOME → ACTION → BELIEFS → IMAGINATION → EMOTION → PERCEPTION.

8. I CAN COACH SOMEONE THROUGH THE CYCLE WITHOUT FIXING IT FOR THEM.

9. I NOTICE WHEN GOAL-SETTING IS REPLACING REAL EMOTIONAL BUY-IN.

10. I HELP PEOPLE REINTERPRET RESULTS SO THEY STAY ENGAGED.

REALITY CYCLE TOTAL: ☐ / 50

SCORE	REALITY CYCLE
40-50	YOU LEAD THE CYCLE CONSISTENTLY
30-39	STRONG FOUNDATION; YOU DRIFT UNDER PRESSURE
20-29	OFTEN STUCK IN OLD LOOPS
10-19	YOU'RE LIKELY LEADING OUTCOMES WITHOUT TENDING THE INNER LEVERS

PART 2: INTERPRETING YOUR LEADERSHIP RESULTS

Leadership Role Totals

ARCHITECT OF POSSIBILITY: ☐ / 60

CATALYST OF GROWTH: ☐ / 60

STEWARD OF OUTCOMES: ☐ / 60

Using the scores from your role totals, rank your three role subtotals:

FIRST (HIGHEST): ________________________________

SECOND: ________________________________

THIRD (LOWEST): ________________________________

- Your **highest** role is your *Nature Zone*—you do it naturally, especially under pressure.

- Your **middle** role is your *Flex Zone*—it shows up when you're intentional.

- Your **lowest** role is your *Growth Edge*—not because you're broken, but because it costs you more.

Your Nature Zone is where you're going to perform at the highest. It's where you have the most capacity to continue to bend and continue to grow. It may sound simple and easy to lean into what you already do well, but most people tend to value these natural parts of themselves the least. And they certainly value it less than those who are benefiting from it. Here's the lens reframe: These natural talents are actually the most important when you consider the fact that *this is where people are benefitting from you the most.* This is where they're getting the most value from you. That's a big deal! So why wouldn't you focus on magnifying that? Why wouldn't you want to build on that impact?

As you lean into your Nature Zone, I want you to also consider your Growth Edge. We're all good at certain things, but we're also really not great at others. That's okay. But ask yourself *why?* Why do I struggle with creating space for new ideas, or working with emotion, trust, and courage, or turning intention into results? What are the dynamics at play here? Is it because what's required here is just so far from your natural hardwiring? Or is it that you haven't been intentional in strengthening these skills?

This ranking also creates your specific blend order from highest Leadership Role to lowest and identifies your BendStyle Type. (For more information on each type, go to Appendix E: The Six BendStyle Types (all-in-one profiles).

ARCHITECT → CATALYST → STEWARD
= THE VISION IGNITER

ARCHITECT → STEWARD → CATALYST
= THE BUILDER-DESIGNER

CATALYST → ARCHITECT → STEWARD
= THE HEARTFELT INNOVATOR

CATALYST → STEWARD → ARCHITECT
= THE CHANGE COACH

STEWARD → ARCHITECT → CATALYST
= THE MOMENTUM MAKER

STEWARD → CATALYST → ARCHITECT
= THE ACCOUNTABLE ENCOURAGER

YOUR BENDSTYLE TYPE:

If you loved this material and want the full BendStyle Profile (Business Edition) experience with a **360 twist** (others can take the assessment about you) and a compiled report, use the QR code below.

THE SIX BENDSTYLE TYPES
(All-in-one profiles)

TAGLINE: You bend reality by opening possibility and lighting the emotional fuse that gets people moving.

What you do best: You walk into stuck moments and make the air feel different—like there are more options than everyone assumed. You create safe space for bold ideas, then pull people emotionally into the vision so they believe change is possible. When you're at your best, imagination becomes normal, courage rises, and momentum starts.

Strengths you can count on

- You generate options quickly and help others see beyond the current story.
- You create emotional ignition—people leave conversations with energy and belief.
- You're a natural reframer: You shift "We can't" into "What if?"

Watch out for these things:

- Execution can lag behind inspiration if no one owns the finish.

- You may over-rely on momentum and under-build systems.
- When outcomes disappoint, you can jump to a new idea instead of tightening the process.

Under stress: You can **stay in inspiration mode**—generating new ideas when what's needed is ownership and follow-through.

Your best move: Make sure every big possibility becomes one small experiment with a clear owner. Your gift becomes unstoppable when it's anchored.

2. The Builder-Designer (Architect → Steward → Catalyst)

TAGLINE: You bend reality by designing the future and building a path that makes it real.

What you do best: You're not just an ideas person—you're a structure person. You can see what could be, then reverse-engineer a path that makes it doable. People trust you because you don't only inspire them; you create plans that prove the vision wasn't hype.

Strengths you can count on

- You hold vision and execution at the same time.
- You simplify complexity into a sequence of next steps.
- You create environments that reward imagination *and* follow-through.

Watch out for these things:

- You can underrun emotion and assume clarity equals buy-in.
- You may push forward while people are quietly unaligned or discouraged.
- Under stress, you can become "efficient" at the cost of connection.

Under stress: You can **over-index on clarity and execution** while under-reading how discouraged, anxious, or disengaged people feel.

Your best move: Don't just build the plan—build the people. Take a moment to name the emotional weather before you execute.

3. The Heartfelt Innovator (Catalyst → Architect → Steward)

TAGLINE: You bend reality by creating trust first, then freeing imagination and new stories.

What you do best: You move hearts before you move plans. You can feel what people are carrying, and you're not afraid to go there. That emotional honesty creates trust, and trust frees creativity. When you're leading well, people don't just perform—they grow.

Strengths you can count on:

- You create psychological safety through empathy and courage.
- You pull real truth into the room without shaming anyone.
- You unlock imagination because people feel seen, not judged.

Watch out for these things:

- Follow-through can be inconsistent if no one converts insight into action.
- You can drift into "processing" when what's needed is a decision.
- You might protect feelings so much that accountability gets fuzzy.

Under stress: You can **keep processing** when the moment needs a decision, a commitment, and a next step.

Your best move: After every breakthrough conversation, ask: "What's one action we're taking in the next twenty-four hours?" Anchor emotion to movement.

4. The Change Coach (Catalyst → Steward → Architect)

TAGLINE: You bend reality by turning emotion into traction– truth, then action, then momentum.

What you do best: You don't avoid feelings—but you also don't get stuck in them. You help people tell the truth, then you help them do something about it. You're built for transitions, conflict, and pressure seasons when reality has to shift now.

Strengths you can count on:

- You normalize emotion and convert it into constructive next steps.

- You're steady in hard conversations and clear about expectations.
- You rebuild confidence through action and visible progress.

Watch out for these things:

- You may solve too quickly and skip the "what else is possible?" phase.
- Under pressure, you can become intensely practical and narrow the horizon.
- You can unintentionally train people to depend on your coaching energy.

Under stress: You can **solve too quickly** and skip the "what else is possible?" expansion that creates breakthrough.

Your best move: Before you lock the plan, ask one Architect question: "What would we try if we weren't afraid?" Possibility expands your already-strong execution.

5. The Momentum Maker (Steward → Architect → Catalyst)

TAGLINE: You bend reality by creating progress fast and improving the system as you go.

What you do best: You're a builder of outcomes. People feel safer when you're around because progress happens. And unlike many executors, you still have vision—you can see what needs to change, not just what needs to be finished.

Strengths you can count on:

- You create traction fast and keep it moving.
- You turn ideas into action without waiting for perfect conditions.
- You refine strategy through results—feedback doesn't threaten you.

Watch out for these things:

- People can experience you as intensity or pressure, even when you mean well.
- You can treat emotion like a delay instead of a data source.
- You may assume others are motivated by the same drive you have.

Under stress: You can **push intensity over connection**, and people may feel pressure instead of possibility.

Your best move: Build emotional buy-in like you build a plan: on purpose. Name what matters, celebrate progress, and invite people into the "why" before the "what."

6. The Accountable Encourager (Steward → Catalyst → Architect)

TAGLINE: You bend reality by holding the standard and the person—accountability with heart.

What you do best: You combine backbone with compassion. You call people higher without crushing them, and you tell the truth without making them feel like a failure. When you're leading at your best, people grow because they feel both challenged and safe.

Strengths you can count on:

- You create clarity and accountability with relational strength.
- You keep people engaged through setbacks by reframing outcomes.
- You're dependable—others trust your follow-through.

Watch out for these things:

- You may stay close to what's realistic and under-invest in imagination.
- You can spend so much energy stabilizing the present that you forget to reinvent it.
- You may avoid "wild ideas" because you're protecting the standard.

Under stress: You can **protect what's working** so much that you under-invest in imagination and bold reinvention.

Your best move: Schedule possibility. Give yourself (and your people) protected space to imagine without immediately executing. Vision fuels your already-strong leadership engine.

ACKNOWLEDGMENTS

eality Benders was truly a labor of love, and like most meaningful things in life, it was not created alone. This book exists because of the talent, commitment, and heart of three extraordinary people who walked alongside me throughout this journey.

Erin, your ability to step into my world of scattered ideas and unfinished thoughts and somehow extract clarity, meaning, and momentum is remarkable. You don't just help organize words; you elevate them. You challenge me, stretch me, and consistently bring out work that is better than what I believed I could produce on my own. Your talent, intuition, and writing style are a perfect complement to mine, and our collaboration has been one of the most rewarding creative experiences of my life. Beyond the work itself, you made the process energizing and fun, even when the path was messy and constantly changing. Thank you for your patience, your positivity, and your belief in this project.

Jesse, you possess a rare kind of creativity and have the ability to see around corners that most people don't even realize exist. You have an instinct for asking the exact question that disrupts complacency and forces deeper thinking. Many of the most important ideas in this book were sharpened, expanded, or completely reimagined because of your perspective. There is something wonderfully unconventional about the way your mind works, and this project is immeasurably better because of it. I am deeply grateful for your insight, your curiosity, and your willingness to challenge the process when it mattered most.

Sarah, you were the steady force that made completion possible. While the rest of us lived in ideas and creativity, you lived in execution, schedules, organization, accountability, and forward motion. You brought structure to chaos and momentum to moments that might otherwise have stalled. Your discipline, consistency, and commitment ensured this project didn't remain just a vision but became a finished reality. Quite simply, without you, this book might still be a collection of conversations and notes instead of something people can hold in their hands. Thank you for your leadership behind the scenes and for keeping all of us moving forward.

To each of you, thank you not only for your contributions to this book, but for your friendship, encouragement, and belief along the way. The relationships we built throughout this process mean more to me than I can express.

There is something just slightly off-center about the way your minds work, and thank God for it.

ABOUT THE AUTHOR

reg Cagle is a passionate advocate for authenticity and a catalyst for transformation. As a transformational executive coach, international keynote speaker, and corporate culture strategist, Greg challenges leaders to confront the invisible forces shaping their organizations, belief systems, emotional patterns, identity ceilings, and cultural drift.

He doesn't believe your success is decided by circumstances. He believes it is engineered from within—by harnessing the power of emotion, reigniting imagination, and unlocking infinite possibilities.

With more than twenty-five years of entrepreneurial leadership experience, Greg brings hard- earned wisdom from building and leading his own companies. Greg has partnered with organizations such as McCormick & Company, Planet Fitness, Steel Dynamics, United States Army Special Operations Command, and the U.S. Food and Drug Administration. Across industries—from five-star hospitality to manufacturing, from technology to higher education—Greg challenges leaders to think differently and act boldly. His global experience spans New Zealand, Australia, Singapore, Italy, Spain, the United Kingdom, Germany, Canada, and Mauritius, where he has coached executives and leadership teams to build cultures that blow away the competition.

As a longtime executive coach and speaker, Greg combines practical leadership frameworks with bold imagination—helping leaders achieve breakthrough results in business and in life.

While he now coaches executives around the world, Greg's passion was forged in the quiet moments of rebuilding his own identity—learning firsthand that before you can bend an organization's reality, you must first bend your own.

ENDNOTES

1   M.B. Dastagiri, "Universal Laws, Nature Laws, God Laws, Spiritual, Philosophical & Science Laws: Origin, Rationales, Prophesy, and Human Well-Being," European Scientific Journal 20, no 8. (2024): ESJ Humanities, European Scientific Institute, doi:10.19044/esj.2024.v20n8p26

2   Robert Cialdini and Melanie Trost, "Social influence: Social norms, conformity and compliance," The Handbook of Social Psychology, ed. D.T. Gilbert, S.T. Fiske, & G. Lindzey (New York: McGraw-Hill, 1998), 151-192.

3   President John F. Kennedy Moon Speech at Rice University on May 25, 1961. https://www.rice.edu/jfk-speech

4   Alikay Wood, "Dolly Parton on the Prophecy That Shaped Her Future," Guideposts, https://guideposts.org/angels-and-miracles/miracles/gods-grace/dolly-parton-on-the-prophecy-that-shaped-her-future.

5   Samantha Kubota, "Dolly Parton Says She Contemplated Suicide Years Ago on New Podcast," Today, NBC News, Oct. 15, 2019, https://www.today.com/health/dolly-parton-says-she-contemplated-suicide-years-ago-new-podcast-t164660.

6   Being Eddie, directed by Angus Wall (Netflix, 2025) netflix.com.

7   Id., 11:46.

8   Id., 18:06.

9   "How Vera Wang Went from Ice Skater to the A-List Crowd's Top Bridal Designer," Women's Wear Daily, Fairchild Media, Nov. 3, 2023, https://wwd.com/pop-culture/celebrity-news/feature/vera-wang-history-1235909839/

10   Rachel Gillett, Business Insider, and Richard Feloni, "19 Extremely Successful People Who Changed Careers After Turning 30," Inc.Com, Nov. 29, 2017, https://www.inc.com/business-insider/people-who-found-success-and-changed-careers-after 30 years old.html.

11   Elise Wachspress, "How to Think About Thinking," Neuroscience News, May 8, 2020, https://neuroscience.uchicago.edu/attention.

12   Kate Douglas, "What Is Thought and How Does Thinking Manifest in the Brain?" NewScientist, May 20, 2024, https://www.newscientist.com/article/mg26234920-900-what-is-thought-and-how-does-thinking-manifest-in-the-brain.

13 https://pmc.ncbi.nlm.nih.gov/articles/PMC7907463/

14 Donald Hebb. The Organization of Behavior (Wiley & Sons, 1949), 62.

15 Akihiro Goto, "Synaptic Plasticity During Systems Memory Consolidation," Neuroscience Research, October 2022: 1-6, https://doi.org/10.1016/j.neures.2022.05.008.

16 Elizabeth Dougherty, "What Are Thoughts Made Of?" Ask an Engineer, MIT School of Engineering, April 25, 2011, https://engineering.mit.edu/engage/ask-an-engineer/what-are-thoughts-made-of.

17 Jill Jonnes, Empires of Light: Edison, Tesla, Westinghouse, and the Race to Electrify the World. (New York: Random House, 2004), 55-67.

18 Ibid.

19 "Edison's Lightbulb," The Franklin Institute, https://fi.edu/en/science-and-education/collection/edisons-lightbulb.

20 Edmund Morris, Edison (New York: Random House, 2019), 384.

21 William H. Meadowcroft, The Boy's Life of Edison (New York: Harper & Brothers, 1911), 301-302.

22 Brendan Harris, "How to Win Every Time" (brendanharris.true.power) Instagram, November 4, 2025. https://www.instagram.com/reel/DQqBqZqkyf3/?igsh=MWRjYnQybWFpNndodw==.

23 Robert W. Gore, The Early Days of W. L. Gore & Associates, Inc. (Newark: Self-published 2008), 129.

24 Terje Grønning. "Working Without a Boss: Lattice Organization with Direct Person-to-Person Communication at W. L. Gore & Associates, Inc.," Sage Business Cases, 2016, http://www.sk.sagepub.com/cases/person-to-person-communication-at-wl-gore-&-associates-inc.

25 Gary Hamel, "Innovation Democracy: W.L. Gore's Original Management Model," Management Innovation eXchange, September 23, 2010, https://www.managementexchange.com/story/innovation-democracy-wl-gores-original-management-model#:~:text=A%20lattice%2C%20with%20self%20managed,located%20in%2030%20countries%20worldwide?

26 "About," Empowerment Plan, https://www.empowermentplan.org/about, accessed December 11, 2025.

27 "How a do-it-yourself windmill project turned into a do-it-for-others foundation for Africa's youth," The Call to Lead: A Campaign for Dartmouth, Dartmouth College, 2021, https://calltolead.dartmouth. edu/stories/difference-between-idea-and-opportunity-space-work-and-mentor-help.

28 William Kamkwamba and Bryan Mealer, The Boy Who Harnessed the Wind: Creating Currents of Electricity and Home (New York: HarperCollins, 2009).